Kristina,

May you always master the "me" in time.

Rock the World,
Jaene
11-16-19
Ch. 4

DEAR TIME

ARE YOU ON MY SIDE?

DEAR TIME

ARE YOU ON MY SIDE?

by Ky-Lee Hanson

contributing authors: Deirdre Slattery, Charleyne Oulton,
Sara Gustafson, Habiba Jessica Zaman, Charmaine Hamp,
Effie Mitskopoulos, Stephanie Butler, Karem Mieses, Yomi Marcus,
Sherri Marie Gaudet, Maryann Perri, Diana Zurbuchen, Tina Kalogrias,
Janelle Mason, Julie Chessell, Falon Joy Malec,
Natashia Newhouse, Jessica Stewart

GOLDEN BRICK ROAD
PUBLISHING HOUSE

Published in Canada, for Global Distribution by Golden Brick Road Publishing House Inc.

www.goldenbrickroad.pub

For more information email: kylee@gbrph.ca

ISBN:

Hardcover: 978-1-988736-61-7

Paperback: 978-1-988736-62-4

Ebook: 978-1-988736-63-1

Kindle: 978-1-988736-64-8

To order additional copies of this book: orders@gbrph.ca

CONTENTS

PREFACE 9

INTRODUCTION 13

SECTION 1 What Is Time? 17

    Defining Time 19
    BY HABIBA JESSICA ZAMAN

    Living Timelessly — Ego & Time
    Are Not Our Enemies 29
    BY NATASHIA NEWHOUSE

    Time Is An Inside Job 39
    BY CHARMAINE HAMP

    Managing The Me In Time 51
    BY KAREM MIESES

SECTION 2 Age Ain't Nothing But A Number 63

    But When Is The Timing In
    Life Ever Right? 65
    BY SHERRI MARIE GAUDET

    The Not-So-Subtle Art Of
    Finding Myself 75
    BY JESSICA STEWART

    Time Is On Your Side 85
    BY DEIRDRE SLATTERY

    Life, Not According To Plan 95
    BY SARA GUSTAFSON

SECTION 3 Fear Is A Time Robber 105

Is My Mind Playing
Tricks On Me? 107
BY EFFIE MITSKOPOULOS

Time To Ditch Your Guilt
And Your Fears 117
BY DIANA ZURBUCHEN

Lost In The Depths Of Time 127
BY TINA KALOGRIAS

The Wait Is Over . . . Your
Time Is Now! 137
BY YOMI MARCUS

SECTION 4 Heartbeat to Heartbeat 147

Change Your Timeline 149
BY STEPHANIE BUTLER

Voices Through Time 159
BY FALON JOY MALEC

The Face Of The Beast 171
BY JULIE CHESSELL

A Premature Lesson In The
Value Of Time 181
BY CHARLEYNE OULTON

SECTION 5 Change The Course Of Time 191

The Sign 193
BY MARYANN PERRI

Six-Minute Increments 203
BY JANELLE MASON

All Of The Things 213
BY KY-LEE HANSON

Preface

WRITTEN BY KY-LEE HANSON

"Books have a unique way of stopping time
in a particular moment and saying:
Let's not forget this."

~ Dave Eggers

Dear Time, Are You On My Side? combines social reality and spiritual reality. On the back cover of this book, I ask a series of questions: Why are we here? Are we happy? Do we have any control over what we experience? Are we the main character in OUR life? Why are we letting ageism affect us; why do we take part in it? Society conditions us to set expectations about age and time, about what life should be, which then blur our self-worth and confuse our very existence. Is it possible to live differently, on our own terms and at our own pace — be it faster or slower than others?

Who made up these rules, anyway?

We abide by time so rigidly when, in fact, it is fluid. Time is a feeling, an expression, an experience that equates to our existence.

This book features women from all walks of life, each with their own successes, trials, and shared experiences: entrepreneurs, ex-corporate hustlers, mothers, professionals, authors. What they share is a collective consciousness of time, and the meaning it holds for each of them. The majority of the population spends their time in the hustle, bustle, and demands of society. For each of our authors, though, various life experiences made them look at their time here on earth more critically and provoked the start of their purposeful journey: *Why is this happening to me? What is my purpose? What is the point of all this? What am I searching for? When can I finally control my own time? What would it feel like to be my own boss? If only I could stop time, then I would _____. What would it feel like to finally live life on my terms? Would my perception of time be different then? Would I then be happy? What is happy? Who am I?*

This book idea came to me in a very *modern* moment on social media. There I was, at my computer, reading comments on a post I can't recall; a woman made a comment regarding spiritual living and that *those people* need to "get back to the *real* world." I sat in thought for some time and then asked her what she meant by "real world" — what is her interpretation of reality? She replied, "Life is not easy and people are trying to take a lazy way about it, we can't create or do as we wish, people need to take part, get a *real* job, etc."

My mind spiraled. I don't look at time or life in this way anymore, but I did at one point in my life. *At what point did I change? At what point did I become more conscious of my being?*

I may be conscious of my existence but I am not a yogi, I am not a spiritual guide. I don't feel "fulfilled" by taking on various socially accepted identities, roles, or titles (boss, woman, wife). To me, the feeling of being proud is better explained as gratitude for an experience and being alive than as a badge of ownership or achievement. Sure, people need to refer to me as something, a name, and I do enjoy words and language. I thrive on how I spend my working hours, and that role needs a title to which people can easily relate. I understand these communication tools and respect their validity within a society. **But those titles aren't me.** Similarly, I love material items; they do give some insight into my comfortability, preferences, and experiences thus far in life. **But they don't identify me.**

I am a being, on this earth, taking part in society. Society does not make up my reality; in fact, society is not a reality at all. It is created superficially with a goal of providing people with an illusion of stability *while under a fog of greed*. There is the saying that if every person took care of one other person, we would all be taken care of. Tribes live in harmony, cohabitation, without greed. We *can* survive and thrive through union instead of competition. The model we are blanketed under is broken. When I think about reality, it sometimes begs the question: Are the relationships we have real, and true? I ask this question because every individual has a different perspective of the said relationship and of each other. We have all been greatly conditioned, and are still finding ourselves. No one will ever see me exactly as I am. I am part of their time here on earth, as they comprehend / see fit, as they are of mine. Two perspectives and experiences can never be exactly the same. This is the most fascinating thing about our existence, each of our unique, precise, and individual views.

What is real, however, is what our soul feels. We are here to feel, to feed into and from, the energy source. We yearn for sacred bonds, but in our society, we don't know how to simply be. To feel without judgement, and only with understanding and curiosity. We have been conditioned to look at relationships and opportunities as "what is in it for *me*?" When I stopped worrying about my own gain and started to be in flow with intuition, people showed up in my life to whom I didn't have to explain myself or compete with. I don't feel they take from me nor I from them.

Instead, we take from the same source, and we pour energy back into it. Every living creature takes from this energy as a whole. We *create* the greater good / great energy, but some people try and deplete it; this is greed. Often people do show up in our lives who look as if they are ready to pour in, but words can be deceiving. Actions tell all. They aren't ready. We don't have to be "careful" and "cautious" of who comes into our life; we just have to point them to where they can take from and how they need to feed energy back into it. When I stopped trying to help individual people and stopped focusing on only helping myself (my raise, my car, my happiness, my need for approval), I saw my effort switch toward a larger source. It is not about individual need and gain; it's about collectively harnessing our energy so we can all live our best life.

The thoughts and teachings in this book resemble Maslow's *Hierarchy Of Needs*. Many people, including the authors in this book, have been stuck in a scarcity mindset, the need for safety. People tend to gravitate to jobs, actions, and lifestyles that fulfill only our basic needs. However, our authors have made progress in moving above the scarcity mindset; they realize that we live in a time, and within countries, where our survival today is likely. We lack purpose when we are living in a state that is already fulfilled; it is time for us to move beyond. When we aren't fighting for our next meal, we can rest, we can relax, our minds can create, and we can alter time. We can clearly think of new and better outcomes. We can get back to our roots and fulfill our purpose of sharing knowledge. As women, we are nurturers and creators, and when we feel safe and secure, we begin to imagine and create peace. We are able to take on more responsibility and to help others feel secure so they, too, can move above scarcity and into love and belongingness, then esteem, and finally self-actualization. When we can take the *time* to realize our time, our potential, our being, we can see that the car, the house, the purse, the job is not what "living" is about. There is no checklist, there are no checkpoints to hit in life. We ARE here to experience, and we are here to share knowledge. We are here to reach a higher being of the self. Spending all of our days feeling constrained by society, feeling the unnatural wants and greed that society tells us we *need*, showing up to a job that is not the right fit for us is all a waste of our time — our life! When we begin feeling our way into things, looking past expectations and comparison, we can begin to live naturally. If we look at life and opportunities as experiences, and not as checkpoints, we gain control over our time. We can experience more things . . . quicker, slower, however we choose. Without the demands of ageism.

Instead of focusing on the fact that half of marriages end in divorce, what about the half of marriages that *never* end? Instead of thinking that your business has an 86 percent chance of failing THIS year, what about the 14 percent chance that you will still be doing this for the rest of your life? We believe what we hear, and we shape our lives around these beliefs. If we start controlling our outlook and erase our expectations of life and time, we will see them take a different form. Things will become more abundant, more plausible, and more possible.

Time is energy, and time is possibility. Time is a common thread we all have. We choose and create each moment through our thoughts, our actions, our words. When we know who we are outside of this body and world, and learn to check in with our self about our experience here, then we can truly become masters of our time. When you are living out your purpose fully and genuinely, then time is a gift, not a burden. We all have the same purpose here, and that purpose is to learn compassion and selflessness, and to be truly happy.

Introduction

WRITTEN BY KY-LEE HANSON

"Let me know when your entire life
goes up in smoke, then it's time
for a promotion."

~ The Devil Wears Prada

If there is one thing we as humans and as a society love doing, it's this: waiting. Waiting to complete a chapter of life. Waiting for approval. Waiting for acceptance or a deal. We wait on other people and situations to change, and we wait for others to give us their approval, the "okay," the green light. We wait for permission to develop into the person we've envisioned becoming. We wait until our environments get so bad that they go up in smoke before we say, "Okay, it's time for a change."

It has been time for ages. Life is made up of ongoing change, but our society resists that, trying to slow it down and create unnecessary processes. All of those checkpoints we robotically need to meet or wait for — the raise, the promotion, the wedding, the home, the children. Instead, we need to give *ourselves* a raise: in time, confidence, organization, money, love, and happiness.

Gaining control over our situations mostly starts with confidence and interpersonal skills. Are you worth these things, a raise in one or more aspects of your life? Everyone is worthy of *their own* time and choosing how they spend it. Everyone is worthy of rising, elevating themselves. Life can stall, and we can feel stuck when we aren't mindful of our time, of where and with whom we are placing our energy. You are worthy of others' time in your life, and you are deserving of removing them if needed, because it is *your* life. Every person is a unique being, on a unique path, creating all that surrounds them. We all play roles in each other's lives, and in the most compassionate way, we need to be the master of what roles people play in our *own* life by defining the relationship. If you feel out of place, you probably are. You could be playing the wrong role. We *can* change that story. Change it! There is no one you owe your time to. Rise sister, rise!

You may be thinking, *What if it is someone else's time that is limited, precious, fragile, or toxic?* We can't control the existence or choices of others, but we can choose how we react, support them, and involve them within our time. We can be the positive to the negative; we can create the balance if *we* are the right fit for that situation.

This book will share stories of gratitude, control, creation, and mind-altering experiences in both past and present moments, and will show how everything that is ticking around you is powered by you. When we learn to grasp our time, which is a creation of our life and experiences, we can practice revisiting points in our life and working them out, creating new solutions, rewriting our story so it affects us differently *now*. We can learn to see life and time as nonlinear. If you are feeling lost, stuck, depressed over the past, anxious for the future, then you are living nonlinearly, but in a scarce way, not an abundant way. When we decide to heal in order to gain new perspectives from past experiences, when we take action to learn new insight, and when we learn how to simply *be* in this very moment while being conscious of what parts of our past and future we are letting influence our now, we can control how our time plays out.

Our authors show you a glimpse into a window of time when they felt frozen, fearful, unworthy, trapped, lost, broken, or at an end. Some of them lived in that reality for years. Many of these feelings we fabricate from the stressors of day-to-day life, from a *reality created for us*. But ultimately we have the power to change, destroy, and recreate that reality. Maybe we feel these negative feelings because we are in fact trapped, trapped in a way of life that just doesn't feel natural *because it is not*, and we judge ourselves for not being able to conform, settle, or be "happy" with simply getting by. *What is "getting by" anyway?* Spending a lifetime in a job that doesn't actually serve humanity, in which you are miserable and suffering? But hey, some people have it worse? Be grateful? I'm not sure spending a lifetime doing something forgettable is what gratitude is all about. I think being grateful is about each breath you take, each kiss you give, each flower you smell, each sunset you watch, each friendship you make, and each time you can share knowledge. Being grateful for your mind and the opportunity to use it. Having gratitude that you can make others smile. If you aren't doing something in your life that gives you this experience, living in a society as we do with an abundance of choice, why aren't you choosing to?

Settling is time poorly spent.

Until you do something about it, you will continue to live the exact same way, repeating the same days and hours, the same lifetime, over and over again, suffering from the ego. Once you take control by letting go in order to open space and fill it with reading, writing, traveling and listening, art and culture, and practicing acceptance, you will be on the path to seeking enlightenment. When you begin to share and spread knowledge, you are reaching purpose. This is the point of life: to seek enlightenment and share it with others. It is up to you to figure out what your "life" embodies.

Now that you may want to pursue the bigger picture of existence, you have two choices: Drop everything and go find it, or weave in the exploration alongside your daily life. This book has been designed as a guide to help you better understand your time, your hopes, your dreams, and your purpose. Along the way, you will have various workbook activities, and at the end of this book, it will be time to write your own story and perspective on time.

Dear Time, Are You On My Side? is the third book in the Dear Women Guide Book series, which Golden Brick Road Publishing House was birthed from. The first book, *Dear Stress, I'm Breaking Up With You,* was followed by the award-winning *Dear Limits, Get Out Of My Way.* My idea with this series was to first address stress from an internal, external, societal, priority, and expectation standpoint. If we come to terms with what stresses us out and how we can reduce that, we will be more clear-minded. We will then have clarity and some strength to face the obstacles that are limiting us, such as our money relationship, our career placement, our fears around standing out and making choices, or leaving our toxic or limiting environments. The books are designed to be read as a stand-alone guide on a specific topic, with each chapter bringing a unique focus and perspective. We designed the series for the busy-minded, the restless, the "give me the answer now" types; we want the reader to be self-serving and to have the ability to jump around the book and focus on what she needs at that given time (a nonlinear approach). After we have gone on a stress-cleansing transformation, have made it through obstacles, and are mastering our time, we will likely be exhausted. Growing pains are a real thing. My three-year journey with these three books has led me to a place of clarity and understanding. I am completely in control of my life, but I am tired. It was a journey to Self, and she is strong and mighty. She required a lot, and now she needs to balance. Next comes time for self-love, so naturally the next book in the series will be *Dear Love,* a strong display of compassion: love, acceptance, partnership, and collaboration. It is not led by me; I have shared the space, and our coauthor Sara Gustafson will lead us on the journey of love. Self-love is born out of a desire to prioritize your time, health and wellbeing, your life above all else so you can serve a bigger purpose.

Time management is about having healthy boundaries, knowing when to set them, when to say no, and when to break down the walls so you are open to receiving. Time management is about more than an organized schedule; to be honest, I am terrible at organizing when it comes to lists and calendars, but I am amazing at showing up and completing what needs to get done. It is about prioritization, being in the right state of flow, feeling into what you are doing, and observing the experience, not worrying about the future or being hung up on something that happened in the past. When we can *be*, we will know this, too, shall pass and we can continue in motion, in many motions and many directions at once. We can be many. Time management is about how you feel in this **current** experience — how *you* feel, not someone else's feelings reflected onto you. Living your life, living your time. Living is an experience. Right now, as our authors have, you might be experiencing exhaustion, substance abuse, anxiety and depression, or the illness of a loved one. You may be a parent to a sick child, your company or career might be collapsing. Maybe you are a single mother trying to start a new career, maybe you were in a loveless marriage, maybe your dreams seem to forget to bring you along, maybe you have moved around the world and feel lost in the loveless, connectionless society that North America instills (because if we were all in a state of flow, we wouldn't need the corporate structure we are caged to and *think* we feel "secured" by), maybe you are feeling so busy and completely out of control of your time or are living your life under someone else (spouse, friend, boss). These can be passing moments, these can become memories, but they do not have to be an identity. They do not have to be your entire life and how you spend all your time. We can use our imagination to visit the past or the future, we can live in states of depression or anxiety, but we can also create states of happiness, and we can imagine desired outcomes. If we look closely at the path to getting there, we can control our time. We can influence the pain around us and write the story.

In this very moment, we are setting up the next chapter of our life. While this book is titled *Dear Time, Are You On My Side?* ask yourself, as you read through each chapter, *Am I on my side?*

SECTION 1

WHAT *IS* TIME?

"Time can be controlled; the setback with things that can be controlled is, they can also control us."

~ Ky-Lee Hanson

FEATURING

Habiba Jessica Zaman
Natashia Newhouse
Charmaine Hamp
Karem Mieses

Chapter 1

Defining Time

---

by Habiba Jessica Zaman

"No one but you can define your
experience or existence."

~ Habiba Jessica Zaman

Habiba Jessica Zaman

——————————————
——

www.habibazaman.com

ig: @habibti_zaman

fb: habibajessicazaman | northstarofgeorgiaauthenticity
· · · · · · · · · · · ·

HABIBA JESSICA ZAMAN, NCC LPC, has a Master's degree in professional counseling specializing in trauma and is the therapist and owner at North Star of Georgia Counseling. With fifteen years of work experience in the counseling field, including counseling, advocacy, guidance, and education, she believes that as awareness of one's fears, perception, desires, and strengths increases, one can make successful life changes. Increasing our self-awareness through becoming more honest with ourselves can initiate the that often results in healing, transformation, and a fuller life. Habiba has thirteen publications that started with a children's book, But I'm Just Playing in 2012; her latest co-authored works, *Beautifully Bare, Undeniably You* and the original *You've Got This, Mama*, were released in 2018. Habiba is of Bangladeshi and American descent. She has two children and lives in Atlanta, Georgia with her family.

Timeless Practice:

◇— What does "time" mean to you? —◇

"What I love most about rivers is: You can't step in the same
river twice, The water's always changing, always flowing."

~ Stephen Schwartz

HOW DO WE DEFINE TIME? Is it based on the number of minutes, hours, days, or
years that have gone by? Or is it based on moments and memories that hold
emotional value? Is time a structured handbook — a blending of the tangible
and intangible that gives us a guideline of where we are versus where we are
supposed to be? Or is it an ever-flowing, ever-present companion that serves as
a non-renewable resource?

We are constantly either in desperate pursuit of time or running out of time to
achieve the milestones that have been written out for us, almost like a prescription
— a lifelong dosage prescribed to us from the society and culture we live in, until
we take it upon ourselves to change the dialogue, flip the script. As you continue
to read my chapter and the rest of this book, take some time to pause and reflect.
Think about the existence you have created and honestly ask yourself, *How much
of this is what I have asked for? How much of my existence reflects a narrative
someone else has written out for me?*

There are the moments when I feel I have all the time in the world to experience
life. And then there are other moments when I feel there simply isn't enough time
in the day to accomplish all that is asked of me. Who decides which of these feelings holds more weight or worth? Time is like a river, fluid and always brimming
with energetic currents, each wave, each current different from the previous one.
The moments that came just before are no longer the same as the moments I am
experiencing currently, just as the person I was earlier today is not the exact same
person that I am now. Time is what we make of it.

Time reflects where we are in life — not just what we have achieved but also the
worldview we bring to each moment. Edward T. Hall claimed, *"In monochronic
societies, including Europe and the United States, time is perceived as fixed and*

unchanging, and people tend to complete tasks sequentially. In polychronic so-cieties, including Latin America and much of Asia, time is more fluid, and people adapt more easily to changing circumstances and new information." As you can see, the meaning and significance of time is subjective to each of us; it is what we make of it, which makes it a social construct. Sociologists define time as some-thing that a group of people create and maintain. Therefore, the socio-cultural norms within which we have been raised, including the geographic location of the society we were raised in, can explain how we understand the concept of time and what needs to be achieved within that time. *That* is how the foundations of our values are created, and we just continue growing and working toward these goals that have been set in place by those closest to us.

We have somehow become slaves to the concept of time as it relates to the sequence of our existence. Logically speaking, we have no say in or control over time. We can always rely on the fact that the sun rises each morning and sets each night, and that this pattern will continue no matter what happens on this earth. Logically speaking, we should consider the rising of the sun and moon to be just another phenomenon, like the rise and fall of the waves. And yet, we are bound to it, driven by it, fearful of what it means if we do not *achieve* within its construct. And typically, we are trying to achieve what someone else has decided that we should want from life. We all know this particular story. We should be married by a certain time, get our degrees by a certain time, have children by a certain age, establish our careers within a dictated set of years — and all of this to mean what exactly? What are we trying to prove or gain as we strive to check off these boxes? Is it acceptance, worth, love? On their deathbeds, many people reveal that their biggest regret was the fact that they avoided following their passions because they wanted to conform to what their family or society had planned for them. My question to you is this: If you are bleeding to make all of these things happen within a timeline written by someone else, if it is not a reflection of what you truly want at your core, then why do you continue to strive for these "dreams?"

Knowing what you are seeking starts with knowing your truth. It's not about "finding yourself," because you are not lost. Your truth is there, buried under all the messages you have been given about what or who you are supposed to be. Your truth has been blurred and buried, forgotten even, because of the so-cio-cultural conditioning and messages you grew up around, such as the way your parents responded to certain topics and other people's viewpoints. As Emily Mc-Dowell stated, *"Finding yourself is actually returning to yourself. A remembering of who you were before the world got its hands on you."*

My question for you today is: What do you want out of life? How many peo-ple do you think truly know what they want out of life? When someone is asked whether they are happy, most people respond one of two ways: "I am happy, it is what it is" or "I want to be happy."

Happiness — a word charged with so much meaning, so much energy. The connotation around this word is usually a sense of fulfillment, of laughter, of energy. But how many people do you think actually know what they mean by happiness? Do they know what their definition of happiness is? No, because they haven't made the effort nor have they dedicated the time and energy to figure out what truly makes them happy, what lights their soul on fire. People's retort is typically, "Why is it so hard to be happy?!" It sounds simple, doesn't it? I want to be happy, we all want to be happy, and we all deserve to be happy. It is a fundamental need that we all desire, and yet it is the most elusive and intangible notion I have ever experienced or tried to work with. Right when you think you have a grasp on it, when it's in your hands, somehow it turns into sand and either just slips through your fingers or sucks you down with it. Either way, happiness is not attainable.

What kind of therapist says happiness is not attainable? Oh, wait, me. Why? Hear me out, and entertain this concept for a moment. Happiness is a construct. It's a state of being, just like time. Can you name any state of being that is everlasting? Is sadness everlasting? Is fear everlasting? No state of being is permanent. And the one thing that we, as humans, have a hard time accepting is impermanence. I could be happy (whatever that means to me) right now, and then I can go home and something can happen and POOF — there goes my happiness.

When we become completely overwhelmed, completely engulfed in our sorrow, depression, fear, anxiety, you name it — when we have an intense emotional response to something that life throws our way — it's very hard to answer the questions: "Are you happy? And if not, what is the point?" Have you ever gotten to a point in your life when you're tired of this existence? Some people may feel suicidal, whereas others may feel fed up of living the same way every single day. In either situation, these feelings and thoughts stem from feeling stuck and feeling uncertain of what we can do to live a happier, more fulfilled life that's worth our time on earth. During times when we are in the stronghold of those intense, negative emotions, we need to have an answer to these questions: What is the point of waking up and going through the routine of getting dressed, getting ready, and going about everyday life? What is the point of coming to my sessions and being present and being emotionally there for other people? What is the point of going home, cooking some dinner, and hanging out with the kids? What is the point of working so hard as a single mama to raise these babies as self-actualized, secure humans? What is the point of managing a thriving private practice all on my own? What is the point of pouring myself into writing another book? What's the point of paying $100 for an Uber so I can take my little man to the Ed Sheeran concert tonight, after a full day of trauma sessions, when my son will probably fall asleep toward the end of the show? What *IS* the point?

I run myself ragged to the bone to fit all these elements of my life into one twenty-four hour day because I am chasing *something*. What does this constant striving amount to? What is the feeling I am desperately hunting and searching for, and hoping to attain in my quest to meet these demands? Also, what am I losing in the process?

Recognizing what the point is helps me determine how much of this pressure is in alignment with my values and what I am working toward vs what society has taught me I *should* be. I am a woman in my mid-thirties who happens to be a single mother, running a beautiful counseling practice, maintaining a household with two sassy kids and kitties, writing books, and creating an identity that goes against the very definition of what a Bangladeshi woman should be. My family is proud of my accomplishments, sure, but laced through those words of praise are also lingering remarks about being alone and unmarried. The strength of my achievements is noted hand-in-hand with the disappointment over my not finding another husband. These messages, along with my own fears about how much I am able to provide for my children, can serve as catalysts to an emotional spiraling of doubt, despondency, and despair.

However, knowing what the point of all of this is can also serve as a reminder of the things you need to do to move on from that emotional state (although this is easier said than done when you're in the grasp of those monstrous feelings lurking beneath the surface at that moment). Recognizing the purpose of your efforts creates a pathway out of this state of being by reminding you of the end goal, of where you want to be. Just like the river, the moment we are standing in is only temporary. Working your way through this emotional rut that I lovingly refer to as my "shit ditch" requires you to first recognize that you have a finite amount of emotional energy that you wake up with every morning. I'll say it again, we wake up with a *finite* amount of emotional energy to have at our disposal for the *entire* day. Have you noticed that if you completely lose your marbles in the morning, because something or everything goes awry, by midday, you are just done? And that's the thing, we have our moments when we lose our temper, but it's typically directed at a person who doesn't fully deserve that reaction. Yes, they may have done something that irritated you, but the response you gave them is not necessarily equal to their action. It may be a rational reaction; however, it is not necessarily worthy of our emotional response. Our emotional energy is like a bag of diamonds. Each time we have an emotional reaction to something, we are just giving them away, or even just throwing them.

For example, it's Friday. My babies come home every Friday from their father's place and just about every Friday, at least one negative thing has happened. They are either close to thirty minutes late or one of them is sick and just threw up all over themselves before they were dropped off. Sometimes they're not dressed or one of them is having a complete breakdown because of something that happened with their father. Other days, it's papers that haven't been signed or the class project that needs supplies which we now have to scrounge for. There have also been days when they haven't been fed, and I only have twenty minutes to get myself ready for work, get them ready for school, and have them reach school on time. These are a few things that aren't in alignment with what I believe should have happened based on the agreements their father and I have in relation to the exchange of the kids. These kinds of mornings wreak havoc with my day and their day and throw us all off our emotional equilibrium. I have this emotional response because I had these beliefs about what should happen, and those values were violated.

In the same breath, I will ask you a question: Why are we surprised when things don't go our way? Why are we surprised when people no longer live up to our expectations? What makes anyone's expectations any more valuable? If my ex-husband and I were on the same page about these values and parenting styles, and respected each other's values, we'd still be married. So, every Friday, for the last three years, I have taken this bag of diamonds, my reservoir of emotional energy, and thrown half of them at him. Why? Does he deserve those diamonds? No, they're mine. They're precious. I only have a finite reservoir for the day, and they need to go toward my clients, my babies, my friends, my home, my pets, etc. They're the ones deserving of my emotional energy. But how many times do we throw our diamonds at people who don't deserve them, or at the traffic, or the weather? Why do we fixate on things we cannot control? And if you go back to the first question I asked you (what do you want out of life?), does throwing your diamonds at things you cannot control lead you toward your definition of happiness? If you want to feel fulfilled, do you get it that way? No. Who is sabotaging my existence? Them or me? You guessed it. Me. What steps am I taking to create a life that reflects me, my essence, my soul, my happiness?

I have always been the black sheep of my family (laughs cheekily). My parents would tell you I have forever danced to the beat of my own drum. I would love to tell you that it is because I have always been confident in who I am and what I want, but that's just not the truth. My life has always been a reaction to a narrative someone else had written for me and my actions, a mere trickle effect of the traumas I endured. I was once in constant pursuit of finding my own worth through the acceptance of my family, friends, society, and for what reason? To finally fit in and belong. You see, I do not look the part of what many would expect based on my nationality, so the feeling of not fitting in was embedded from long ago. I didn't think or process the same way, I did not value what many others did, my life story did not sound like that of those around me . . . I just did not belong. I was once a vivacious child, fighting for what I believed was right both verbally and physically, who was fearless and would set off on adventures with her brother, who made friends with people of all stations in life, who was mischievous and curious about how everything worked and why things were the way they were. I was also someone who came in contact with the cruelties that exist in this world, which finally stripped away all my notions of innocence and worth. Over time, I completely lost who I once was under the shadow of trying to become someone who wouldn't be seen as blemished or broken. I had become a shell without a soul. I formed relationships with people, both friends and lovers, who knowingly and subconsciously perpetuated that state of worthlessness, for without their approval, it was impossible to attain what I desperately sought: to be loved, accepted, and valued for being me. It was after the birth of my second son that I felt hopeless, empty, like I was staring into an endless dark void, because I couldn't answer my own question: What was the point?

What do I gain from killing myself to be the best wife, housekeeper, confidant, lover, friend when he says he never wanted to marry me in the first place? What did I gain from choosing him over me, time and time again, and fighting for him just because it was time to pick a husband and I would not settle for my family making that choice for me? What had I lost in the process of trying to satisfy everyone else with how my life is supposed to be? Even then, is it ever enough? I read once, *"You could lie on the floor and let people walk over you, and some people would just complain that you were not flat enough."* Your life can resemble what everyone else believes it should, and you can still find yourself in the middle of the night wondering, *Is this all there is?* So . . . what is it that *you* want?

Stop "shoulding" all over yourself. Release all the aspects of your life that *should* be a certain way based on what others have defined for you. That just creates judgment and self-loathing. No one can define your experience or existence other than yourself. Instead, accept where you are and who you are in this very moment with grace, give yourself compassion for what you need right now, and then focus your energy on who you want to become. Just as you cannot step in the same river twice because the water is always changing, you, too, are in a constant state of change and growth. So work toward who you want to be and what you want your existence to reflect based on your own values. Treasure your diamonds and only share them with those who are deserving. Whether it be your time, emotional energy, love, or influence, remember that it is a privilege for someone to receive these gifts from you. No one is entitled to you. Define your own construct of time that is as unique as you. Remember, what you have to offer, the way you would offer it, with the essence of you, no one else possibly could. There is no comparison.

~ I dedicate this chapter to my two amazing boys,
Ryu and Luca, who helped teach me that not only
do they deserve the best version of mama,
but that in order to be able to give them that,
I first have to recognize that
I am worthy of loving myself, too.

CHAPTER 2

Living Timelessly — Ego & Time Are Not Our Enemies

BY Natashia Newhouse

"Imagine how powerful it could be if
collectively, we chose to lock arms and
embrace our uncertainty with
possibility instead of fear."

~ Natashia Newhouse

Natashia Newhouse

aletheiaislove.com

ig: @aletheiaislove | fb: @aletheiaislove

· · · · · · · · · · · ·

NATASHIA NEWHOUSE IS AN ECLECTIC, FREE-SPIRITED SOUL who thrives on creative expression. She is a mother, artist, writer, and intuitive medium from Osage, Iowa. Natashia is the founder of Aletheia, a unique business designed to assist those who seek to explore a deeper sense of purpose and self-awareness. She is licensed in massage therapy, esthetics, and nail technology and holds certifications in reflexology, microdermabrasion, and Reiki. She owned a day spa for many years and now utilizes the knowledge she gained in the spa industry to offer a well-rounded approach to self-care and personal development. Natashia has a deep appreciation for metaphysics, particularly energy exploration and psychic development. She believes intuition is inherent in everyone and aspires to create a safe space for others to develop their own connection.

Natashia enjoys thinking and creating from an abstract perspective. Her art is reflective of this and is often described as a visual representation of energy itself. She loves the emotional response she feels when writing poetry and attributes much of her self-expression to "working out ideas" through the written word.

Natashia has two beautiful daughters and is grateful for every new experience motherhood has offered her. Together they enjoy cooking, traveling, reading, and spending time with friends and family.

"Maybe you are searching among the branches,
for what only appears in the roots."

~ Rumi

"I DON'T HAVE TIME." I'VE UTTERED THIS COMBINATION of words more than I'd ever care to admit. After my beautiful, independent, spitfire daughters entered this world, it became my personal mantra and one that I declared with nobility and righteousness. It was my personal sacrifice to put myself last. Making a martyr of myself — for my children, for their father, for my clients, and for any other person or pursuit that could potentially feed my insatiable desire for approval and acceptance. I reached my thirties achieving many of the milestones laid out on the timeline expected of me, including the completion of college, business ownership, an engagement, and two wonderful children. I had all the possibility of a bright future ahead of me. But something was missing. I couldn't face it directly at the time; to even question it meant I was ungrateful for a life that many would give anything to have.

Had I become so obedient to the construct of time that I'd missed out on actually living my own life?

Time is defined as many things. A quick search on dictionary.com will yield over fifty different definitions of the word itself. Time permeates every corner of our life, but we take its effects for granted. We can't see or feel it, or experience it, with any of our senses, yet all our memories or aspirations require its measurement. We have created ideals, common goals and ways of experiencing them, and when someone or something isn't in alignment with "our way" of time, we pass judgment or often avoid certain experiences altogether. Something has occurred within our society that I believe is often overlooked. We have let the tool become the master instead of mastering the tool itself. And this master has become the driving force behind everything we believe we are "able" to experience.

How often have we looked at a never-ending to-do list and longed for something more meaningful? How many engagements with friends and family have we declined simply because of the guilt we harbor for not accomplishing those things we left unchecked on the list? How many years have we endured a job that provides no sense of purpose or fulfillment, while dreaming of how amazing it would feel to pursue something that actually excites us? How often do we feel pressured to follow the societal norms: college, marriage, and kids or even in more subtle ways, such as our health and appearance or by following the same daily schedule that all who have come before us have rigidly adhered themselves to? These were the questions I began asking myself. My life was not lacking by any means. I had experienced hardships along the way, but I felt I had applied them in a sense that provided growth. *What was my problem then? Was it all in my head?*

It actually was, and the timing of these specific questions brought me face-to-face with my mind's own construct. The ego.

The ego has received a lot of attention in recent years. It's often regarded as the "unruly stepchild" or an aspect of the self that encompasses the less-than-desirable thoughts and feelings we have. Without proper attention, it is capable of throwing a nasty tantrum, creating massive destruction in whatever path it chooses. There's a plethora of information available to "keep your ego in check," and it's not uncommon to hear someone say, "My ego got in the way." We have compartmentalized this portion of our mind so much so that we're not even considering it to *be* a part of ourselves anymore.

I invite you to throw this concept out the window.

While our ego gets a bad rap, the soul, on the other hand, is considered the saintly servant. It is the essence of our being and the core of our purity and goodness. Whatever the ego lacks, the soul redeems within its true nature. What if, instead, we could consider the *ego* to be the saintly servant *of* our *soul*? The courageous aspect of ourselves that diligently observes our surroundings and reports back to the soul, with the intent of bringing about the best possible outcome. What if its purpose is to guide us along the way? To provide growth and a way of experiencing life with a unique richness that only each person, individually, can fully comprehend.

The ego is both free will and growth. But it is being stifled by all the information that is paraded before it at any given moment. Historically, it served as a means to keep the hunter safe. Before technology, the mistakes and achievements of others served as examples of what to avoid and how to survive. We now live in a time when we can reach out across the world to witness the experiences of others, even long after the event has occurred. We can learn about absolutely any topic we desire, simply by pulling up the information on a hand-held device. Our ego is on information overload, and if we continue to interpret our new world with old concepts (greed, individualism, sexism, ageism, fleeting time, control, and third dimensional living), the potential to live in a perpetual state of fear will only grow stronger because we are blocking our ability to receive, understand, and expand into the new dawn. We must consciously download this information and be aware of our rapid growth in the process. We can take the events and circumstances we indirectly experience through our technology and expand upon them. Our awareness can give us the opportunity to grow and solve problems in a new way and with an unlimited amount of resources. However, we have to make the conscious decision to sift through this information to find the resources and solutions that are of the greatest benefit. We do not have to accept that any of the misfortunes of our world cannot be changed or that they must be avoided.

Consider a somewhat extreme but important example to explain the information overload theory: When we learn any new skill, we rely on repetition to solidify our understanding and ability. The ego works in a similar way. We log onto Facebook and witness the recorded events of a mass school shooting. A week later, another mass shooting has occurred at a mall. A day later, yet another mass shooting takes place at a public event. The ego recognizes the growing threat of mass shootings. The circumstances are unpredictable and could occur at any location and at any moment in time. Our ego then becomes fearful and interprets all its surroundings in that context. As we go about our day carrying this underlying fear, we don't trust our surroundings or the people we encounter. We find reasons why we shouldn't go to certain places or interact with certain people. This trickles out into other areas of life, and a blanket of distrust forms over everything. Nothing is safe from the unpredictability of our world. We retreat to familiar, predictable places, while feeding our ego's desire for information by relying on the access we have at our fingertips. We stop directly experiencing and we overlook the good we encounter because the ego is so saturated and aligned with the bad that has been forced into its perception.

By no means am I suggesting that the threat of mass shootings isn't very real or that ignoring the information altogether will solve the problem. But in its extremity, this is a good example of how the ego can be influenced by its environment and how it can then apply its perception to other areas of life. The more evidence of something presented before it, the more solidified that "something" becomes. Violence has been brought to our attention and the evidence suggests the potential to encounter it is exceptionally high. But these incredibly powerful circumstances in our life also open up the opportunity to become aware of everything great our world *does* have to offer: unity, empathy, kindness, joy, love, and possibility. We can adopt certain measures in an attempt to prevent or eradicate as much of any threat as possible, but I believe the long-term, concrete solution lies within each individual taking accountability for the type of energy they are projecting out into the world. Our true power lies within our ability to embrace diversity. Extend a helping hand to someone in need. Embrace someone for their uniqueness and remind them why it is so beautiful. Allow others the space to define themselves and find ways to build *up* their confidence, rather than tear it *down*. Imagine how powerful it could be if collectively, we chose to lock arms and embrace our uncertainty with possibility instead of fear. Perhaps then such dire circumstances wouldn't even become a part of our reality because we wouldn't have allowed it to accumulate such an extreme charge of energy. I believe our ego simply needs some redirection, and with this redirection we can begin to utilize it to its fullest potential.

Consider for a moment: if our soul is connected to the source of our being (such as God or any other term we may use to describe it) and if our source of being is constantly in a state of *perfection*, then what purpose would our ego or time really serve? If a state of perfection exists, so does a path to get there. Time and ego, as they are traditionally understood, would only serve as roadblocks along such a path, operating almost as a means of punishment for those who are unable to discover what the "correct" path is. The belief that we must prove ourselves worthy of achieving an epitome of existence only perpetuates more lack, limitation, and unworthiness. But the "epitome" is personal and defined individually. Because so many individual definitions exist, I don't believe the source of our being is at any state of perfection or completion. I believe, in my entirety, that our source is in a constant state of becoming. It is our purpose in this lifetime to experience growth, and collectively, we propel this state of *becoming* through our own individual experiences. We then utilize time as points of reference, weighing events of our past against our present and then applying them to the future. The purpose of our ego then becomes apparent; it is a faithful assistant who gathers information to direct us forward. Ego and time walk hand in hand as tools for either success or failure.

I held the belief that things needed to be "horrible" before change was necessary, a belief I had to let go of to fully understanding my own circumstances. This limiting belief prevented me from making changes because things weren't "bad" enough or I could appear to be taking something as important as my children for granted. I had gotten wrapped up in my own checklist, following the timeline of something that was supposed to guarantee success, to the exclusion of what my soul actually longed for. I did want a partner, children, a successful career — all a straight shot to happiness with minimal blocks along the way. But while I was so busy ensuring I didn't disrupt the status quo, I forgot to check in with myself to see if it actually worked for me.

My former fiancé and I had an accidental pregnancy after a short time of being together. It was a beautiful accident that led to so many other amazing experiences in life. However, we were so programmed to believe having children together meant the next step was marriage; not to mention, we were approaching our thirties anyway so settling down per "society's standard" seemed the next logical checkbox to tick off. We stopped acting like partners and focused on living the right way, at the right time. My career also suffered. I had spent years and thousands of dollars on schooling to get to the position I was in. But the excitement and passion I once held began to dissipate because I hadn't even asked myself if the work I was doing fulfilled me in any way. Here I was now, in circumstances and at an age when a person typically stabilizes their career, their path, their life, and I wanted to begin a completely new career. It was terrifying and something I believed, wholeheartedly, I did not have the "time" to do.

Time means different things to different people. Personally, it was the ticking clock that ultimately represented endings. I was racing against it to get things accomplished before it was too late. I never had enough of it; there were always too many tasks expected of me and not enough hours in the day to complete them. The playfulness and creativity of a child had already expired and the success and wisdom of an elder hadn't yet been afforded to me because I was in my thirties. Time had brought me to this point, in my present, because it did not want to be confined in the same way I had been confining myself. Like a river containing too much rainwater, its fluidity was aggressively rushing over the banks and spilling out onto all areas of my life. It was creating an ocean out of my stream.

It took a lot of unraveling and asking myself a lot of the right questions to get to the core of what I was feeling. My ego witnessed the path of least resistance. It took all the information presented to it from my childhood on, and directed my thoughts and feelings to what it believed was the best possible outcome. Essentially, I should have kept my ego in check, but not from a place of idle awareness. I had to take my own experiences and expand upon them. I had to have the desire to step out in a new direction, with a willingness to embrace the unknown, while transitioning the ego out of its former perceptions. Once my ego and I reached a state of cooperation, outdated concepts fell apart and things began to change. I began to find room, and "time," within my mind to consider other possibilities. This ultimately led to the breakdown of the time construct. I realized the quality of my life was not dependent upon the number of hours I spent in college or choosing the "right" type of career. What mattered was that I was pursuing something I felt passionate about, that gave me the drive to show up and utilize my strengths to the best of my ability. The love I felt within my relationship was not based upon my marital status or what type of "provider" we could be for each other. It was based upon our connection and our willingness to provide space for each other to be our authentic selves, even if that meant marriage didn't actually work for us. My effectiveness as a mother was not dependent upon my ability to put myself last but rather on setting an example for my daughters of what it really means to be an empowered woman. My position on the timeline didn't matter; what mattered was that I had decided to become conscious of where that timeline led me.

Beneath the ego and the restrictions of time, our soul feels its way through existence by emotion. We are drawn to certain things by the way we feel, and the ego lets us know what sort of success we can expect from its bank of similar information. The first step is simply to acknowledge those feelings before the internal dialogue begins regarding why we should or should not do something. Intuition is inherent in all of us and if we allow ourselves to feel it, we generally know what it is we truly desire, despite the influence of anything external. When we shift our focus internally, we begin to ask the right questions. It has been said that the only moment we ever truly possess is the present, and I believe this to be absolutely correct. Our present moment stands as the pivoting point between the experiences of the past and the creation of the desires of the future. If we are too busy utilizing the present to tear ourselves down for past mistakes or to project fearful expectations into the future, we forfeit the position as master of our own life and experiences. Time is capable of becoming our greatest ally rather than the mysterious entity we're racing against to arrive at our desired destination. Instead of viewing it as something were competing against, we can bring our awareness into the present and allow time to work for us. Every single moment in time represents the opportunity to make a choice. We can base these choices on the meaning we associate with time — its historical representation to us on both a personal and a social level — or we can choose to forge our own path. Time is fluid and the possibilities are endless. If we step into the possibility of joy and love, our ego will guide us to greater experiences of such joy and love.

Life is a gestalt of rich, captivating, and dynamic moments. It is not a series of lucky accidents or unfortunate events. I believe it is our birthright and responsibility to define our capacity for growth by thoroughly and irrevocably experiencing each of these moments with every ounce of our being. We are meant to evolve, expand, and explore. We are not meant to discover everything that the world lacks, hide from its possible ramifications, and then pass judgment against anything that does not fall into this perspective. Each person is in their own stage of growth and with growth, we experience forward movement. Resistance often feels as though we aren't moving at all, but I believe that the more we resist this movement, the greater it builds, until we have no other choice but to move forward. We can determine how painful or joyful our growth is by becoming consciously aware of the choices we actually desire. I have decided to stop resisting. I pause and ask questions whenever I feel the tug from my soul to choose a different direction. I have decided to move with the Universe and with this cooperation, it no longer feels the need to thrust me into what I once believed was unknown territory. The duration of difficulties I encounter has shortened because I choose to be aware of what I am grateful for, instead of what I fear. I am no longer racing against time and have found joy within the spontaneity of living my life from the present moment. Our lives are a unique way in which the Universe expresses itself. To deny any moment that uniquely belongs to each of us is to deny the Universe its own expression.

Let's start living. There's no better time than right now.

~ To my father — thank you for always taking a chance on my "big" ideas, even when it made you lose a few hairs, dollars, and nights of sleep. Your faith is only surpassed by the amount of love you've given me.

CHAPTER 3

Time Is An Inside Job

BY CHARMAINE HAMP

"Time is well spent in silence while observing your thoughts without judgement."

~ Charmaine Hamp

Charmaine Hamp

www.meditationalbirth.com

ig: lovealchemy11 | fb: meditationalbirth

· · · · · · · · · · · ·

CHARMAINE HAMP IS A CATALYST FOR CHANGE through LOVE ALCHEMY Coaching. Growing up in minus-forty degree temperatures on the prairies of Canada, she learned how to create love and warmth for everyone with whom she came in contact. Charmaine has a strong desire to help people, so she naturally pursued the field of medicine. After one year of pre-med studies, she sensed the large gap between helping people heal and prescribing them medicine. Charmaine left her medical studies and Saskatchewan behind and moved across the country to Montreal to learn French. She was eventually hired as a fashion model by Ford Models Toronto. She traveled the world as a model and then went on to pursue her love of the arts at Stella Adler Acting School in New York. She graduated with the lead role in the acclaimed Broadway play, *August Osage County*. From there, she accepted an invitation to the Los Angeles program for Film and Television. She now calls Los Angeles home.

Charmaine uses all her experiences, including her acting training, to take the stage in many different capacities. Her primary love is seeing people step into living the life of their dreams through her work as a life coach with LOVE ALCHEMY Coaching. She teaches self-love workshops and is a motivational speaker in Los Angeles and around the world. She is also a kundalini yoga instructor, author, and a HypnoBirthing® coach, inspiring beautiful, often pain-free births.

WHAT IS TIME AND WHY DO WE ALWAYS FEEL LIKE WE DO not have enough of it? What if I told you there is no such thing as time? Our logical minds understand time as something that is real, but our souls know that we are immortal and have an abundance of "time." How does this possibly make sense in a rational world, this world of reality?

Our cells are constantly operating in the present moment. They go right to work from the instant you think or speak a thought. Creation lives on the tip of our tongue. Therefore, we must stop complaining. When we keep repeating that we that don't have enough time, the Universe goes right to work putting up obstructions in our way. Why? Because we have been given the gift of creating our own reality. When we complain about our lack of time, we are actually creating a lack of time for ourselves.

Start by making a simple adjustment to your thoughts by using these simple mantras:

"I am making more and more time for myself every day."

"I have so much time on my hands to pursue my goals and dreams."

"I have more than enough time to be super successful at achieving all of my deepest desires."

"I am a powerful creator."

"I have so much abundance coming in easily and effortlessly that I now have more time for leisure and play."

"I use my time wisely and efficiently."

These are just a few examples of affirmations you can use in your daily affirmation rotation. When you begin to change the neuron pathways of the brain with affirmations and carve new belief systems, you will witness your life rapidly change as more time and opportunities open up. Then you can create new affirmations that lead you through the next part of your journey to further you on your path toward fulfillment.

Make a list of the things you desire in your life. This will provide you with clarity and save you a lot of time and energy. For example, I saved a lot of time on dating apps by writing out what I wanted in a partner. I was also able to quit my waitressing job and start living the life of my dreams by writing down exactly what I wanted in my dream job. My list of characteristics in an ideal partner reached 250 things by the time the love of my life came in and he turned out to be everything on my list. My dream job list was up to 200 items before the restaurant I was working at caught on fire and burned down. I had no choice but to start working on my dream job: helping people thrive as a life and wellness coach while becoming a yoga and meditation teacher and a HypnoBirthing® coach.

Remember you can be, do, and have anything. You are creating this life. If you don't believe me, check this out: You are a product of the last five conversations you have had. Speak into creation the life of your dreams.

If writing a long list sounds daunting to you, you do not need to sit down and write it all at once. As you walk around in your daily life and you see something you desire, add it to your list. Do not give attention or judgment to the things that do not suit your fancy; pay attention only to the things that you would like to include. Speaking our words and writing them down catapults our desires into action. You can also start every morning with a simple list of everything you need to accomplish for the day. If you don't get everything completed, don't criticize yourself — just put it on the top of the list for the next day. When you look back at your life and your lists, you will see that there was nothing that was ever *so* important that you *didn't* finish on time.

Another wonderful way to clear the mind and open up more space in your life is to free write. Free writing releases internal emotions that wreak havoc on the heart. Once we get our worries, fears, and doubts on the page, they no longer plague the mind and we can get on with our day. You can either do this in the morning if you have some alone time or at night before you go to bed so you can clear your head for a restful sleep. For twenty minutes non-stop, write down every uncensored thought, whatever comes to mind. Take on this practice for forty days and see what kind of time opens up for you. Forty days is the amount of time it takes to make or break a habit according to yogic traditions. A forty-day meditation or yoga practice can open up time by clearing our mind.

Now let's examine the idea that our soul is immortal. Consider the idea that we have more than one life. Perhaps whatever it is you are going through at this time is happening for your greatest and highest good. Imagine for a minute that your soul selected your journey because it knew you could overcome whatever challenges you would face. It knew that you were always in the right place at the right time. Any discomfort or challenge in your life has been set up to give you a gentle push in the direction of your soul's highest calling. The Universe is trying to help you with a wave of contrast to propel you toward your dreams. So the next time you feel like a roadblock has manifested in your life, look around and try to find the lesson that may be hiding in your story to propel you in a different direction.

"What was the best time of your life? If you can say right now, it is because your inner life is fulfilled." ~ Deepak Chopra

When we are completely in the present moment, we are operating from a space of no worries, no doubts, no fears, and thus no time.

Think of the last time you had an orgasm; you were completely in the moment. You were not thinking about what you were going to make for dinner or that business deal that was waiting for you on your desk. You were so in the moment it felt like time disappeared. *These* are the moments when your deep desires come to fruition. *This* is how we create beings / babies and how we become mothers / fathers. We are constantly creating or birthing something yet sometimes, we waste our precious time creating things we don't want by worrying about things instead of clearly asking for or stating what it is we do want. This is one HUGE question I ask myself, *all the time*, when my mind begins to go off in all directions: *What do you want, Charmaine, what do you really desire?* We get so caught up in the world of negativity, creating our life from a place of fear and scarcity, that we hinder ourselves from moving forward. As a result, we don't get anywhere.

It is like the cab ride theory. If you get into a cab and you do not know where you want to go, you may say, "Uhhhh turn right, oops I think I meant turn left. No, wait, can you do a u-turn?" We end up wasting a lot of time, money, and energy. Society and early programming from family, friends, neighbors, schools, etc. have driven home the habit of thinking about the *worst possible outcome* instead of thinking about the *best possible outcome*. For example, next time you think of asking for a raise, instead of thinking of all the bad things that might come from the experience, only state the good things that will occur from it. Focus on things that your boss will say: "I am so glad you came in today. I have been meaning to take a closer look at everything you have done for the company and yes, I believe it is time to increase your salary. You are a valuable asset to the company. I appreciate everything you have done for us." Keep these thoughts in your mind until you walk in the room to have your meeting and watch how the meeting unfolds exactly as you stated. When we realize we are constantly creating our reality, time unfolds easily and effortlessly for us. We create more time with each powerful thought about how we would actu-

ally like to see our lives unfold from the most loving place for ourselves and others.
"Put your hand on a hot stove for a minute, and it seems like an hour. Sit with a
pretty girl for an hour, and it seems like a minute. THAT'S relativity."
~ Albert Einstein

When we are happy, time flies. Therefore it is important to start from a place of
happiness. How do we do this? It starts from the very moment you wake up. Think
of all the things you are grateful for. If you don't know where to start, begin with
the fact that you woke up to another day. You can find gratitude for your bed, for
your pillow, for the partner next to you, or for the beautiful space you are creating
to call in a partner. Gratitude creates latitude.

*"What you focus on expands, and when you focus on the goodness in your life,
you create more of it. Opportunities, relationships, even money flowed my way
when I learned to be grateful no matter what
happened in my life."* ~ Oprah Winfrey

If you have been struggling with finding peace and more time in your life, repeat this powerful mantra by Sadhguru to yourself over and over throughout the
day, twenty to fifty times: *"My dominant intention is to feel good."* This mantra is
powerful enough to shift your life. Words have meaning. They carry energy with
them. This is why it is important to watch the thoughts you are thinking, the words
you are speaking, and the stories you are telling. Become a constant observer of
your life and you will create more time in the direction you would like to see your
life evolve.

Were you told that you had to work hard for a living? Most of us were fed that
belief because that is how mass society thought and how it continues to think. As
a result, people found they had to work hard. Are you starting to get it? Did anybody tell you to work with joy in your heart? Did anybody tell you that your work
can and should express your passions and your love? Unfortunately, most of us
believe the tale that we have to work hard, *painstakingly hard.* And we go through
life doing just that: working hard, eating, drinking, procreating, and eventually
dying without experiencing what our true purpose is and why we came to earth at
this time. We have a certain amount of time and a certain amount of energy in our
lives, and unless we use it with joy, we are missing out on the simple truth of life.

What are we working for? To get the new car, the dream house, the dream
job, etc.? Sadhguru says that in life, we are always trying to acquire more things.
But even when we acquire everything we want, there is still something missing.
This is the desire to feel good. All a human being wants is to feel good. We also
must realize that at the end of the day, humans will always desire more. Once we
understand this, that is when both time and space open up with grace and ease.

It is important to understand that we will always desire more so that we can keep creating. When we truly desire something, when we want something bad enough, and it manifests itself with ease in our lives, we still seem to get stuck on the hows. "Now, how is this going to happen?" For example, let's say you are unhappy with your job; all of a sudden, you get offered a new job, but it's in New York. Now you have to move to New York. Naturally, you start stressing about the "how." How will you sell your house? Where will you live in New York? How will you afford it? Instead of getting stuck on the "how," understand that the Universe is a thousand steps ahead, bringing the right people to you to buy your house, to find a home that is close to your work, to make the money to pay for the relocation, and on and on. Trusting in the Universe creates time. Trusting that this life is here *for* you and not against you opens up a world of possibilities.

"Don't seek, don't search, don't ask, don't knock, don't demand — relax. If you relax, it comes, if you relax it is there. If you relax, you start vibrating with it." ~ Osho

The practice of meditation plays an important role in creating more time. It connects us to our soul's clarity. It brings us inner peace and develops our intuition, our inner knowing. Meditation helps us release any unconscious, time-wasting habits, subconscious fears, or blocks. It helps promote clarity and brings balance into our lives. The most successful people on the planet have learned to meditate and incorporate it into their daily success rituals.

If you have never meditated and have no idea where to start or have tried to do so but have given up out of frustration, don't fret. Many people, including myself, have found it difficult at first. It is often challenging to quiet the endless mental chatter, but without daily practice, the mind will find every excuse not to quiet down. There are a number of ways to meditate. You do not have to just sit there. Find the right way for you. Be easy on yourself. Start with three minutes a day and build up from there. You can do a walking meditation connecting in nature. Study a tree and notice how it is in constant meditation. You can take a class or go to a yoga studio where meditation is part of the practice. Not every way will be right for you, but as Yogi Bhajan says, *"It is our excuses that are our self-abuses."*

"You should sit in meditation for twenty minutes every day — unless you're too busy. Then you should sit for one hour." ~ Zen Proverb

By implementing a daily meditation practice, we are clearing out intrusive thought patterns to purify our minds and get on with our goals. We also learn not to judge our thoughts but rather to be the constant observer of our thoughts, watching them come and go. This in itself will change our lives. The more we become aware of our thought patterns, the better chance we have to shift and heal our lives.

"The mind is beyond Time and Space. It is part of the Universal Mind. It is given to you as an instrument to serve you. What happened? It becomes your master, you become the servant. The mind becomes a monster when it becomes your master. The mind is an angel when it is your servant. It is all in the mind. The meditative mind is a purely beautiful state of living." ~ Yogi Bhajan.

When our minds control us and govern our thoughts and life, it is difficult to get to a space of fulfillment. Being fulfilled is what time is all about. The key to this fulfillment in life is self-love, to feel good, and to find joy in all aspects of life.

In order for us to cultivate self-love and truly find joy, we need to tune into the desires of our soul. We need to tap into our present moment — the discomfort and the ease. We must realize that every moment is a call from the Universe to foster greater awareness of what we truly desire in our lives. In doing so, we become the conscious creator of our reality through our thoughts, words, and actions.

~ Dedicated to Gloria and Helmut Hamp. To my parents and all parents who support their children in the pursuit of their dreams. It is with their unwavering love and support that I have been able to pursue every career leading up to my purpose. The whole way through they encouraged and supported me. I owe my life and the healing journeys of many others to them. Love is the greatest force of all. Thank you, I love you Mom and Dad!

Timely Practice:

◇— What do you want to manifest? —◇

What are 10-200 characteristics of that desire? What does that job, person, situation, lifestyle, personal state look and feel like (the more words, feelings, emotions, and visualization you put into it, the more you create the clarity you need to find it and bring it into your life):

....

....

....

....

....

....

....

Chapter 4

Managing The
Me In Time

BY Karem Mieses

"We need to make better DECISIONS with
the time we have, not get more time."

~ Karem Mieses

Karem Mieses

Start at karemmieses.com/deartime

ig: karemmieses.official | fb: karemmieses

• • • • • • • • • • •

KAREM MIESES IS AN INTERNATIONAL MANAGEMENT CONSULTANT with a proven track record of success in process improvement, corporate profitability, and new markets development. Since 1996, she has been helping companies optimize their resources and mitigate their risk using her diverse educational background and multicultural influence. Karem has the unique ability to align a company's vision with operational initiatives, enabling companies to achieve breakthrough results.

Nonetheless, after the birth of her third child, her life took a different turn for the sake of her health and that of her son. She developed a system based on Six Sigma principles and project management principles to upgrade her life, help corporate clients optimize their performance and scale their businesses, and help families lead an active and healthy lifestyle. Her motto is: If we can measure it, we can change it.

Losing fifty pounds and sustaining that weight loss led Karem to help others dive deep into their own transformations. Since 2012, Karem has helped hundreds of people upgrade their lives through fitness, joyfulness, and habit management with her commitment to helping other parents attain a sustainable work-life balance through duly researched, no-nonsense strategies.

She has a bachelor's degree in accounting and a master's degree in management of science and technology and has received several business awards for her involvement and initiatives in the business-to-business community, including "Outstanding Women" in the Puerto Rico Senate, "Most Wanted Business Women" by *Business Puerto Rico Magazine*, and "Top 400 Locally Owned Companies" by the *Caribbean Business Magazine*.

ARE YOU LOOKING FOR A BETTER WAY TO ADEQUATELY MANAGE YOUR TIME? Do you feel there is a better way to check everything off your to-do list, leaving time to spare? Maybe you want to conquer your schedule and stop feeling like you are playing catch up *all the time*. If you are anything like me, you just want a sliver of time to chill without an ounce of guilt, while still feeling accomplished.

After working as a project manager creating drastic corporate transformations for two decades, I had figured out how to make everything work for everyone else but myself. *How could I possibly be so good at getting things done (as per my peers, not just my ego) within the work arena and yet feel so unaccomplished in my personal life?* I became obsessed with the process of time management to get things done better and faster and still have time for myself, but I lost track of how fast time consumed itself independently.

You see, time is a paradox in itself. The more we fixate on controlling it, the less effective we become in mastering its use. We cannot manage time, nor can we control it; instead, we can only manage ourselves and *our* use of time. Time is defined by a set variable of given units; no one can have more or less in a day. We are all bound to the same self-ruled playing field of existence. In our effort to rule time, we ignore its ephemeral properties. Trying to manage time is like trying to control air; a whole science is required, and in many instances, even divine intervention plays a role.

But though we cannot control time, no matter how many books we read or courses we take, we can find satisfaction in managing ourselves. Managing our actions is simple, yet not easy to implement. As humans, we tend to look for answers everywhere except within ourselves — because let's face it, *we* are never the problem. Add to that the socio-cultural appropriation and indoctrination of having no distinct boundaries between our work, business, and personal life, and it is no wonder we fall short whenever we want to master something so personal and existential as time.

The philosophies of time management all come from the corporate school of thought in which personal matters are of no concern. Nonetheless, regardless of what we want to attain — say, a promotion, a new business, additional income, better health, or better relationships — it all emerges from the need to feel and achieve a certain level of accomplishment. It is important to note that all achievements arise from the desire to satiate these basic life requirements:

- comfort

- variety

- significance

- love / connection

- contribution

Hence, the key to successfully managing ourselves is understanding not only *how* we want to feel, but *why* we want to feel a certain way. Use the list above to help you discover what you desire so you can be aware of *how* you want to feel when you take on certain ventures in life, and these feelings or emotions will be your breadcrumbs that guide you to take inspired action.

Any traditional time management approach must incorporate personal aspects, including feelings, to lower the risk of disappointment. Checking off tasks on a to-do list and jamming every second of our schedule with events we do not feel connected to or engaging in ventures that lack real purpose is a surefire recipe for mental and emotional burnout, as well as disappointment. It is both ineffective time management and poor self-management.

Before I give you steps to help you manage your use of time, it is critical to understand how our personal affairs intertwine with work, business, and other commitments. It is challenging to compartmentalize work and life when there is no work stability in this new world of globalization. The concepts of "manage yourself," "self-management," and "manage the use of your time" are all intertwined as multiple strings of the same thread. Let's unpack this a bit. Time management has one objective: allocating time slots or chunks to various activities strategically and efficiently to achieve specific goals or outputs in a methodical and controlled manner. Conversely, self-management is the art of mastering and controlling one's behavior by taking ownership of one's current circumstances, including one's well-being. In the end, we have to focus on habit formation to efficiently manage the use of our time.

Don't Fall Into THE TRAP — Five Myths Of Time Management

Let's debunk these time myths to increase our productivity and better manage the "me" in time.

Myth #1 — We have to be good at everything.

Ever heard the saying, "Jack of all trades, master of none?" Yes, that's right, it is impossible for a human being to excel at absolutely everything. We will, of course, excel at what comes naturally to us, and we can do our best at whatever else it is we take on. Successful people learn what's necessary to move their life forward, and this includes things that may not be a part of their natural affinity, but they focus on what they do best, first.

Life is imperfect by nature; as such, so are we. As humans, we all have a unique set of talents and skill sets that come to us easily. For the skills that aren't easily within our zone of genius, we have to apply ourselves that much more so we can excel and master them.

Choose to focus on learning one new skill every three months. This removes the pressure of needing to be perfect and also helps you apply yourself accordingly. By year end, you will have mastered four new skills.

Myth #2 — There are not enough hours in the day to do everything we have to do.

We all have the same twenty-four hours in the day; whether we consider ourselves successful or not, that is a fact. It is up to us to prioritize the most relevant activities to move our business and lives forward and to make peace with letting go of activities, people, or ventures that do not propel us forward.

It's not about your time, it's about your *energy*. Studies show that a person has a decision bank of 200 decisions per day, regardless of the hours available. After that, the brain tells you, *I'm done*. When brain power, or "cognitive load," is maxed out, decision fatigue sets in! Cognitive load1 is the enemy, not time.

We do not need MORE time; instead, we need to choose how and what we dedicate our energy to and make better DECISIONS with the time we have.

Myth #3 — Asking for help is a sign of weakness.

Successful people rely on support systems comprised of key people and systems that allow them to grow, expand, and enjoy life. When we have a vision and focus on the few things and habits that will take us closer to materializing that vision, we become aware of the tasks that need to be delegated, outsourced, or purged.

Asking for help and delegating become essential to expanding our reach. Yet so many of us refrain from doing so. Some of us assume that "Nobody does it as well as me" or "This will end up being more work for me", while others may have the unconscious fear of missing out on all the "merit badges" that work overload provides.

---

1   Sweller, J. (June 1988). "Cognitive load during problem solving: Effects on learning." *Cognitive Science 12*: 257-285.

We need to become better visionaries and leaders of our lives to not only delegate but to inspire our support system to be the best version of themselves at all times.

Myth #4 — Hustle and hard work are necessary for success.

If this were true, there would be more wealthy, happy people in the world. Most of us have been raised under the false belief that success only comes to those who work hard — blood, sweat, and tears included. With this illusion subliminally drilled into our consciousness, we then wear the badges of hustle and busy as an honorable title and live by the motto: If we take downtime or even relax a little bit, we are being selfish.

Our life's work is the product of our habits — not incessant activities, but the right activities. Habits can induce, modify, or destroy our state of mind. On the positive side, habits can also be created, modified, and broken in a matter of weeks![2]

We need to establish better rituals that include rest and recreation to put our mind at ease.

Myth #5 — I have too much on my plate.

The rest of our life will be lived in a constant state of incompletion. However, don't mistake being "a work in progress" with being "overwhelmed." Feeling overwhelmed is usually the result of simply saying "YES" too much and/or a lack of clarity as to what we want out of life, career, or business.

You can clear your plate without guilt by realizing that *success isn't getting everything done, it's getting the right thing done at the right time — and saying no to everything else.*

In fact, your most important job is deciding what will not get done.

By debunking these five myths, your mind should be open to considering unconventional possibilities in which you can control what you do with time.

Five Steps To Successfully Managing The Me In Time

I have always been *that* person — you know, that go-to person my peers reached out for help with projects, papers, and studying for tests. It was a badge of honor every time that my friends wanted me to be a part of their team or requested my help for school projects.

As I moved up the corporate ladder and eventually owned my business, I became the go-to person to "get things done," from implementing new software

---

2   Graybiel, Ana M. (2008) "Habits, Rituals & the Elevated Brain." *Annual Review of Neuroscience 31*: 359-387. Available at https://pdfs.semanticscholar.org/3c1b/bfc46bae-961cbc8c79dec143e1c9775e803b.pdf

company-wide to handling change management in mergers and acquisitions. I do not say this to sound presumptuous but rather to reassure you that I've been doing this successfully for a long time. I urge you to consider this framework with an open mind and, above all, an open heart.

I could easily jump in and give you a "how-to" list, such as how to take an inventory of time, find your perfect day flow with the right scheduling, and even reverse engineer your goals from twelve weeks to a year. However, there is greater value in giving you the steps that all my clients have missed when they land on my door. I have used these steps to help both them and myself stay committed to the productivity habits and project plans we work on together.

Step 1 — How do you want to feel?

We stop doing things because we don't like how we feel. Think back to a point in time when you quit a job, decided to move, or made another drastic change. Maybe that time or instance is occurring right now as you read this book, looking for a guide to control time.

The first step in taking charge of our time is deciding how we want to feel and what we want more of in this *one* life, *our life*. My personal and professional experience over the years has proven to me that when we are looking for change, it is because we are running away from a feeling that makes us uncomfortable or inadequate.

Take the time now to identify those negative feelings. Ask yourself this question: *How do I want to feel for the rest of my life?* Write down what surfaces in your heart and mind. Limit your answer to three power words that embody those feelings for easy recollection.

◈

◈

◈

Step 2 — Change your internal narrative.

Usually, when we are ready to launch a new venture, go for that promotion, move to a different city, or start something new, those negative voices start creeping up inside our head! In psychology, this is referred to as our inner critic, also popularly known as thought gremlins.[3]

---

3   Carson, Richard David. (2003) [1983]. *Taming your gremlin: A surprisingly simple method for getting out of your own way* (Revised ed.). New York, NY: Quill. ISBN 0060520221.

I have found that by reframing the inner critic's comments before embarking on any pivotal life change, I have sufficient leverage to defeat self-limiting beliefs. When we least expect it, those thoughts will show back up, and we should be ready to send them packing (or at least to the back seat) — no negotiations!

For instance, when I hear my gremlin start the pity party, repeating, "Who do you think you are? This is too much for you," I say to myself this power phrase: *This is a sign that I should do this! God is bigger than my problems.*

Now it is time to write your power phrase by filling in the blanks:

"When the negative voice in my head says _____,

I will say back _____. This is non-negotiable."

Step 3 — Write down everything you love doing.

It is time to start digging deep into all those projects and ideas that you have. This simple brainstorm is going to allow you to select the projects that have the greatest chance of overall impact so that you are able to stay focused on them. No more half-completed projects that leave you feeling unaccomplished. Write down everything you love doing, are passionate about, or cannot stop talking about. Focus on the things that would make you agitated if someone "stole your idea." Contemplate the things you would regret not doing one to five years from now.

Use this writing prompt for inspiration to get your creative flow going:

"I am freaking awesome at _____ ,

regardless of _____ ,

because I always can _____."

Now list all of your interests, loves, and passions.

Step 4 — Assess your skills.

If you are like 90 percent of my clients (and me), as you went through the list of the things you love, you probably questioned yourself about whether or not to put them down on paper (the gremlins, yikes). Notice if any of these thoughts came up: *How am I going to do that?* or *Who am I to do this?* or the always famous *What would my mom (spouse, friends, etc.) think?*

No one can help you move past these mental blocks but yourself. Go back to step 1 and revive the feeling that you want to live by. For example,4 who says . . .

- A structural engineer cannot have a dance studio, the #1 ballet school in town?

- An overweight music teacher cannot be a group fitness instructor?

- An accountant cannot be the best bike builder in town?

Allow yourself to imagine and write down two things from your list (step 3) that would be crazy cool to do, to become, or even to have as your main source of income. Next, draw two columns and start making a list:

Why am I good at this?	Why can't I do this?

Once you commit to something, you will gain the confidence to let go of the things that may not get done. It may feel scary as you get more years of experience because it may feel like starting over. However, with practice, you will unleash the power to completely reinvent yourself at any stage of life.

---

4   Case Studies from KEMM Group LLC customers

Step 5 — Honor your non-negotiables.

It is time to focus on the few things that we excel at and the habits that will move us forward. One of the most important habits that we can master to reach massive transformation in life is to determine and honor our non-negotiable activities for the week.

Our non-negotiables are the activities that we have to do daily or weekly to move our life, business, or career forward. The success of these variables does not necessarily depend on how many times you do them but rather on setting a consistent flow for their execution.

Use these questions as guidelines to decide on your non-negotiables:

Is this activity congruent with how I want to feel?

Would this activity get me closer to where I want to be?

Is this activity allowing me to serve or connect with my tribe?

When establishing your non-negotiables for the week, set goals per activity by weekly repetition and the amount of time per week that each activity requires. For example, I don't create content daily, although you will see daily content from me in all my social media platform. I set a goal for content creation of four hours per week, to be done in one sitting; this is when I create batch content.

When we don't have clarity on all these steps, it is very likely that we will end up surrounded by a collection of half-completed projects, good intentions, and another great idea soon to be somebody else's profitable business.

But that is not going to be you, because you have this book in your hands. I want you to reclaim your time by exploring the timeless being within yourself, so you can confidently and purposefully commit to non-negotiable habits and activities that will allow you to master the "me" in time.

~ To my boys, Joel, Xander, Max & Andres, you are my everything.

SECTION 2

AGE AIN'T NOTHING BUT A NUMBER

"Time ticks only to the beat of your attitude."

~ Ky-Lee Hanson

FEATURING

Sherri Marie Gaudet

Jessica Stewart

Deirdre Slattery

Sara Gustafson

Timeless Practice:

◇— What do you feel too old or too —◇
young to do?

◇— Why? What lead you to have —◇
this belief?

◇— Are you ready to change —◇
this belief?

Chapter 5

But When Is The Timing In Life Ever Right?

BY SHERRI MARIE GAUDET

"I believe the most important contribution to my success was my unshakeable belief that I would make it work, 100 percent, no matter what. I didn't always have the answers as to how, I made numerous mistakes along the way, but I would tell myself sometimes a thousand times a day that I would succeed and always believed it wholeheartedly."

~ Sherri Marie Gaudet

Sherri Marie Gaudet

www.lifestyleofsherrimarie.com

ig: Lifestyleofsherrimarie | fb: SherriMarie

. . . .

SHERRI MARIE BELIEVES YOU SHOULD ALWAYS LIVE IN THE MOMENT. She is positive to a fault and will always find a way to make even the most boring task fun. She is all about finding the good in even the worst of situations. She loves to have fun but understands there is a time and place for everything in life. Sherri Marie loves being around her friends, both new and old. She can walk into a crowded room full of strangers and within a few minutes can be found chatting away, forming new friendships. She has always been one who sets her mind to something and, no matter how hard it is, will find a way to accomplish it.

Although she didn't always know what she wanted to do when she grew up, Sherri Marie always knew she wanted to be someone who helped people. Always a risk-taker, often doing before thinking, Sherri Marie believes that nothing in the world is impossible. She thrives and does her best work when the odds are stacked against her. Sherri Marie tried out various career paths during her twenties before finally realizing that her talents were best spent helping others as an entrepreneur and business leader.

Sherri Marie is a national market developer / recruiter. She strives to help people believe in themselves and design lives they love.

HAVE YOU EVER DARED TO DO SOMETHING THAT, when reflected upon in hindsight, you had absolutely no business doing at the time? I opened my salon in January 2008. My crazy idea — "Dad, I want to open a salon!" — had become a reality! I won't lie, ten years ago, I had NO business opening a hair salon. I might have been a "hairdresser," but I think I would have only been considered a "good hairdresser" if it was in a bloopers competition. Honestly, I could probably make you pee your pants laughing if I showed you some of my #TrueLifeHairMasterpieces (more like catastrophes). But even though I was ridiculously lousy at hairstyling and haircutting, I had this huge goal of opening a salon.

Less than a year after graduating hairdressing school at the young age of twenty, and while I was pregnant with my son Brady, I decided that I no longer wanted to be a hairdresser. Instead I wanted to open my own hair salon and run the business side of things. I wasn't the most talented hairdresser, I certainly didn't have the most experience in the industry, and owning a business wasn't my expertise either. But I just knew in my gut that I could run a successful salon; the vision I had for it was stronger and much bigger than my doubts or lack of certain skills. I talked with my dad about it and within three weeks, a building right down the street went up for sale, we made an offer, and they accepted. I closed on the building that would become my hair salon three days after having my son. The building I purchased had previously been used as a dental office, and a very outdated one at that! We needed to completely tear the building down and redesign it into a hair salon.

I didn't tell many people about the building I had purchased or about my ideas to turn it into a hair salon, but the few people who did know had one thing in common: They all thought I was completely nuts. Twenty years old with a newborn baby, and I had just purchased a building to turn into a hair salon when I wasn't even a talented hairdresser. Talk about self-limiting beliefs!

I have never in my life been more proud to be called nuts. Ten years later, when I look back on things, I couldn't be happier that I paid no attention to all those who doubted me — my efforts, my success as a business owner. So many people think small; they think within their comfort zone, sticking with what is safe instead of pushing the limits and following their dreams, regardless of how "crazy" it looks or sounds to others.

There is never a perfect time to do anything in life, no matter what it is. There will always be a million reasons why, instead of jumping in fully and going all in, you hold yourself back. When I decided to open my business, the timing could NOT have been more imperfect. I had just given birth to my son — that alone would have been reason enough to say, "As much as I want to do this, it's just not the right time." But when is the timing in life ever right?

Often when we think about owning a business, it's a typical stereotype that we need to have our life completely in order, have all the seed funding, have all the answers, and possess the perfect skills in our chosen industry. *That* fact couldn't be further from the truth — I am living proof! I was a hot mess express. Yet I have managed to be successful. I always remind people of the saying, "Your vibe attracts your tribe." You will attract people who resonate and re-late with you and your style. Perfection is completely overrated in my book. Be you and do things that make you happy. Stop spending excessive amounts of time trying to be who you *think* you need to be, and just be yourself! Being an entrepreneur is certainly not for the masses. Entrepreneurship will test you for all you've got; there will be obstacles, there will be highs and lows, yet that is a journey that entrepreneurs will gladly go through because of the sense of purpose and fulfillment they gain from following their calling, their happy path. However, even for entrepreneurs, many who are starting out feel as though they need to "blend in" and be like everyone else. They need to look professional and create this perfect brand. They think they need to have the perfect photos, the perfect website, the perfect background, the perfect outfits, the perfect home, the perfect life that they can show off online, and of course the perfect social media presence. They feel like they need to fit in with all the coaches, hair stylists, and makeup artists. Guess what?! When you do this, you actually *lose* the most powerful part of what you have to offer. Think about this for a minute: What if your *uniqueness* is what will make you successful? What if being yourself unapologetically has been the one thing missing from your business this whole time? It does not matter if you use fancy fonts, have just the right colors, or cre-ate a perfectly centered logo. What matters is how people feel after spending time with you. Do they get excited to work with you? Do they want to buy from you? Success is not found only in the serious hustle and grind. No, real success also includes the playful and creative parts of yourself and, most importantly, being authentically you.

When I first decided to open my salon, I knew exactly who I wanted to hire as part of my team; they were the girls I had been working with before I launched my own business. The man whom we had worked for was less than nice to everyone. When I presented them with the opportunity to join me, all the girls wanted to come with me and work alongside me. To say I was excited would have been an understatement. However, I quickly learned that nothing in life worth having ever comes easy. Sometimes things are a great fit, but the timing isn't always aligned. The owner found out about our plan to leave and fired everyone on the spot. My salon was not yet ready to open its doors to the general public, and my potential employees had clients who needed to be tended to. Another salon offered them a job, and they all took the job offer, as they should have.

I have always lived by the motto, "You can never give up on your dreams, even when nobody else but yourself believes they can come true." At the time, I had many people in my life who were pressuring me to do the "logical thing" by selling the building, making a small profit, and becoming an employee at an already established salon. It would have been easy to quit and give up on my dreams when I went from having a full staff of employees to none, especially since I was a young mom with a newborn baby and almost no hairdressing skills. I could have easily sold the building with the renovations we had done and reaped a profit. That would have been the safe and easy road — the road which, in my opinion, is completely overrated. Instead, I hired a seasoned hairdresser for a month to train me one-on-one, expanding my hairdressing skills from "subpar at best" to "hairdressing being second nature."

Remember the saying, "You always had the power my dear, you just had to learn it for yourself?" Although I have always had the ability to persevere and achieve my goals, when my salon opened, I lacked the confidence I needed to implement my vision and lead the salon the way an owner truly should. In hindsight, it's clear that I was my own worst enemy and self-sabotaged my efforts by doubting myself, my talent, my ideas, and my drive for results. I always knew I wanted my salon to be unlike anything else around, a place where people weren't just "employees" but truly important pieces of the puzzle. The first nine years of my business, I didn't make moves without making sure I had approval from all my employees. Doing so led to many ideas fizzling out because getting ten employees to agree on something was almost an impossible task. Additionally, I let people's opinions of how old or experienced an owner should be get inside my head. I wanted my customers to feel not just like customers but appreciated and like they were visiting a home away from home. When I first opened my salon, I hid the fact that I was the owner from my customers. This was not because I wasn't proud of the place; rather, it became a learned response, especially after having numerous people say, "You're the owner? You look way too young to own this place." I started doubting myself; my self-confidence and belief in myself as a business owner took a huge hit. Whenever someone would ask me, "Who owns this place?" I would immediately reply, "My dad." After all, it wasn't like I was lying to people; his name is in fact on the building I own. He played a huge role in ensuring that my dream became my reality. If it wasn't for my dad, I wouldn't have had the resources to create my business; for that, I have been and always will be beyond grateful. I know that not many have the opportunity to take a vision and run with it. However, while my dad provided the financial resources to take my vision and bring it to fruition, *I* was the one who made it into what it became. Looking back now, I wish I believed in myself the way I do today, now that I am ten years older and wiser. When someone recently said, "You look too young to own a salon," I confidently responded, "Age is just a number." I might have been the youngest person at my salon and had the least amount of experience, but I had the biggest vision and I was able to create something they never did.

Confidence forms the backbone of an awesome life and a successful business. I believe we are all born with confidence in ourselves, but certain life experiences can cause us to lose that confidence and question our unique talents and abilities. Eventually, you will be called to own your confidence and get over your past experience, which is how both I and my business grew exponentially. I like to say that my salon and I evolved together. Was it always easy? Hell no! Did I make mistakes along the way? You better believe I did! Did I have days I wanted to quit? 100 percent yes, I did! Did I have people leave, especially those I never thought would leave? Yes. Ironically, I wouldn't change a thing because it was all part of what makes me who I am today and also what makes my salon the place it is today.

When I first opened my salon, I truly believed with all my heart that every employee who started with me the day I opened would stay with us until retirement. To say that I was naive would be an understatement. I had this belief that if I treated my employees like they were important pieces of a puzzle that completed my salon, I would have the happiest employees and the smoothest running business around. One of my biggest visions for the salon was ensuring that not only was I financially stable and growing but that my employees were thriving financially as well. What I didn't ever anticipate was that I would create employees who felt entitled. I learned that having a business is actually a lot like raising children; you need to find balance between being their friend and being their boss. Because I was treating my employees too much like friends, they didn't respect me or listen to me. I would say something as simple as, "Let's all park on the side of the building so we leave the parking lot open for customers." It was something I said to benefit them — a cluttered parking lot is not inviting to potential customers. But just like with children, because I didn't enforce the rule strictly, they didn't follow it, no matter how many times I said it.

Around this time, I also started diving into personal development. As I did, I began to evolve as a business owner. I went from not wanting anyone to know I owned the place to sharing my accomplishment and business baby with utmost pride. I was starting to not just own my salon on paper but to truly own it through leadership and making decisions that *I* felt were best for the business.

Things had never run more smoothly at the salon, but just like anything else in life, I had to expect the unexpected. My central air conditioner broke in the middle of summer during a heat wave, and the wait time to have a new system installed was six weeks. During that time, I lost employees I never thought would leave and once again, I had people in my life doubting me. They doubted whether I still had the passion needed to rebuild the salon because I had also started other businesses and was working on my career as a published author. But for me, failure is never an option; when someone doubts me, when it's sink or swim, the only thing I know how to do is prove them all wrong.

When I had to rebuild my salon eleven years after opening it, I realized something super simple that I wish I had realized when I first started: Age doesn't define you at all. As the months went by and I was succeeding in my salon rebuild, I quickly realized that people reacted differently when they learned I was a thirty-one-year-old salon owner than they had when they found out I owned a salon at age twenty. When I first opened the salon, they would tell me I was "too young" and automatically assume that it had been handed to me. Yes, I got help, and I will forever be grateful for my dad and how he helped make my dreams a reality. Many successful people in life have gotten help in the beginning stages of a business — it is almost like a rite of passage. However, help alone doesn't build a business for you; it is your determination and willingness to do whatever it takes to be successful that builds a thriving business.

The most important factor in my entrepreneurial success was my unshakeable belief that I would make it work, 100 percent, no matter what. I didn't always know how, and I made numerous mistakes along the way. But I would tell myself that I would succeed, sometimes a thousand times a day, and I always believed it wholeheartedly. I wasn't afraid to get resourceful when I needed to, and I was never afraid to make connections and reach out to other successful people for advice, pep talks, and many vent sessions. I spent hours researching how to run a successful business in general and then specifically how to run a successful hair salon. Most people think you have to "wait" before starting something, which is rather silly. If you have a dream or a goal, you owe it to yourself to honor that dream or goal and not let anyone or anything stand in your way. If I was able to do this when I was twenty years old with a newborn son, no previous business skills, and subpar hairdressing skills during one of the worst economic downfalls in recent history, and then again start from scratch eleven years later at age thirty-one, it is proof that success truly is attainable for anyone who is willing to do whatever it takes. Age is just a number — what matters most is your determination, passion, and unshakeable belief in yourself and your abilities.

~ This chapter is for my dad . . . who didn't just believe in me 100 percent from day one, but made sure my dreams came true.

Chapter 6

The Not-So-Subtle Art Of Finding Myself

BY Jessica Stewart

"Go out into the world and learn as much as you can, give back, and love with everything you have, because in the end, that is all that matters."

~ Jessica Stewart

Jessica Stewart

www.yournewbf.com

ig: j_annestew

. . . .

An adventurer from a young age, Jessica has lived many lives in her short thirty-five years. Daughter, sister, girlfriend, wife, student, bartender, explorer, make-up artist, altruist, interior designer, feminist, yoga teacher, and aspiring coach and wellness advisor. Jessica's spectrum of interests runs wide, something she attributes to her restless soul and a deep-rooted belief that you shouldn't have to have only one passion in your life.

At age thirty-three, she found herself divorced and directionless. So she hit the road on an adventure to rediscover herself and her passions. Her journey is a never-ending pursuit to live her best life while helping others do the same. She shares her experiences, good and bad, in hopes of positively affecting anyone she comes across along the way.

Now focused on building a brand to support women like her across Canada and beyond, Jessica is focused, happy, healthy, and working through the shit every day. Through great tragedy comes great clarity, and the end of one thing is only the beginning of something greater. Her goal is to help others see the same, chase their passions, discover who they truly are, and live one hell of a good life.

MY FAVOURITE GAME TO PLAY RIGHT NOW IS "GUESS MY AGE." I like this game not as an ego boost or as affirmation that my skincare is worth all the money I pay for it and that my vegan diet is paying off, but to prove a point about society's view of where you should be in your life by a certain age. I play this game because I do not let the number of times I have circled the sun define who I am or what I can do. I play it because it is only human for most people to judge your age not only by how you look but also by how you act and what your circumstances are.

This past summer, on my thirty-fifth trip around the sun, I had people guessing a good ten years younger than my actual age. Society's skewed perception of time implies that we should be living the lives of our parents and possibly even our grandparents. In this perspective, I should be married with two and a half children and established in a steady career by my age. But in reality, on my thirty-fifth birthday, I was managing a bar for the summer in cottage country after spending six months vagabonding in California. Working at a seasonal resort is something most people would do in their twenties. Well, here I was, well into my thirties, renting a room in a cottage, working my buns off, and having the time of my life. Should I get judged for that? No. But I was. This, I believe, solidifies my viewpoint (and confirms I will continue to spend money on skincare).

But who was judging me? While I definitely got a few eyebrow raises when I told people what I had been up to, it was mostly my own ego judging me and projecting those judgments out as fear. Fear of disappointing my parents, fear of what others might think of me, and a general fear that someone was going to call me out on it: "Jessica, you aren't a child anymore. Stop acting like one!"

Society places deep-rooted expectations on us as we age. Go to school, get a job, get married, have babies, raise children, retire, maybe travel, and then die. But be sure to do the steps by the time that is deemed age-appropriate; otherwise society will think you have lost your mind, feel sorry for you, and form other preconceived notions about you. I am here to tell you that is a load of bullshit. Where in there did anyone say, "Make sure you are happy?!" Now, lucky for me, since I have always liked to push the envelope and go against the grain, I've always been open to finding out who I truly am. So I decided to take my happiness into my own hands, rather than entrusting someone else with it.

I got a job as a bartender right out of high school, not knowing what else I wanted to do. I dated a little, drank a lot, got into a long-term relationship, bought and sold some houses and cars, played grown-up for a bit, went back to school in my late twenties, got a career, got married, and got divorced. Let me say that again — divorced. Thirty-three years old and divorced. That was not in the plan. As much as I like to push the limit, subconsciously I still had expectations for my life and where it was headed, and being single in my thirties was not part of that vision.

There I was, alone and not knowing who the hell I was. My plans, goals, and direction were not applicable anymore. My best friend just left me, and I was lost. I had buried myself in my relationship and had been more worried about taking care of my husband than myself. It was a strange place to be, and I felt very lonely, especially because all my friends were married and having babies and seemed to have their shit together. I realized I didn't know who I was, what I wanted, or where I was going. Some people would feel sorry for me and tell me what an asshole he was for doing this to me, but truth be told, he gave me an incredible opportunity. He gave me a chance to start over again, to discover who I was as an adult and who I wanted to be. To explore, meet new people, and do things I would have never done if we were still together.

I quit my job, put my stuff in storage, packed my car with the essentials and my dog, and chased the sun south. I took time to write, explore, reflect, surf, do yoga, and meet new people. Some days I cried thinking about how my life had failed, but most of the time, I was just genuinely happy. Something I had not felt in a very, very long time. I didn't realize this until I finally had a moment when I looked around and couldn't help but smile as everything made my insides happy. Pure bliss.

But amidst this happiness, my perception of time would creep in and slap me in the face. Holy shit, I'm thirty-five years old, and I am acting like I am twenty-five. *What is wrong with me? What are people thinking of me? Shouldn't I be working a nine-to-five job, counting down the minutes until happy hour on Friday, and repeating that week after week until I am allowed my scheduled two weeks of paid vacation for the year? I should be making dinner for my family and taking the kids to soccer, not sitting on a beach watching the sunset alone.*

That is what society tells us: You are too old to act this way. To that, I say f*ck it. My happiness is driving *my* metaphorical bus, and this life is not a *one-size-fits-all adventure*. I soon came to the realization that the only person I truly had to answer to was myself, and that in itself added to my happiness. I stopped trying to do what everyone expected me to do and followed my heart to happiness.

Trust me, this is not as easy as it sounds. We want our friends and family to be proud of us, not to think we are crazy. But it takes courage and strength to live a life that some people (let's be honest, most people) do not understand. Courage to step outside the box, out of your comfort zone, and outside the norm. Courage to truly find out who you are and what makes you happy, at any age.

Forget the norms. Forget your age because it truly is just a number. Forget what everyone around you is doing and what they think you should be doing. Everyone is put on this earth to write his or her own story, which means comparing your path to someone else's is detrimental to the screenplay that is your life. There is no timeline that works for everyone. This is your one life to live and explore as you see fit.

Now I am not suggesting you do what I did. This is my path. Quitting your job and living out of your car across the country doesn't work for everyone, but it worked for me. Just focus on living your life in a way that makes you happy and at home with yourself.

Living your truth at any age can be an internal battle that constantly needs to be fought. Like any self-work, it is not something you can decide to do one day and then not have to work to keep yourself moving forward. I work on this every day. I battle my demons, some days more than others. Some days, my inner voice screams at me,

WHAT ARE YOU DOING?

Do you really think this was the right move?

Did you need to quit your job? Was that the responsible thing to do?

Should you have left your home?

Are you acting like a child?

Are you ever going to grow up?

You are on the down slope to forty, is this how forty year olds are supposed to act??

But then I stop, take a breath, and think of the life I have created and how happy I am. I am figuring out who I am more and more with every passing day. I am taking the time to appreciate where I am, the people in my life, and the opportunities I have gained instead of spending my weeks in the hamster wheel running on autopilot and waiting for the weekend. *Would it have been better to stick it out and live a life I hated or to take the leap and a little more time to find something that truly lights my soul on fire?*

* * * Most people I talk to are not happy with their lives. Typically it's a work situation; they feel trapped, thinking they are too old to start over again. This could not be further from the truth. The old dog is never past learning new tricks or stepping out into the discomfort zone. Perhaps the older you get, the more planning it takes to change things up, but never rule it out.

There is no law that says you must have A, B, and C completed by XYZ year and that if you miss the deadline, sorry, you are out of luck and must suffer in the regret of the what-if's. What if I had just taken the chance and not worried about what anyone else was thinking of me while I did it? Because guess what? Chances are, they don't care. And if they do have something to say about it, it is only because they are envious that you had the courage to live your best, most fulfilled life.

Time can be a thief of joy. If you count it too closely, it can ruin your experiences, and if you pay it no attention, it will rob you of your life. What I am trying to say is this: Your life is going to fly by whether you like it or not. So take the time to be aware, be conscious, and seize every moment. Don't run on autopilot. Take deep breaths, look around, and take in all the beauty that surrounds you. Take every opportunity that comes your way. Do not be afraid of change; embrace it. We all have the chance to start again, but not all of us will take it. Too scared, too ashamed, too worried that others will think we are too old, too fat, too young, too skinny, too confused, too hurt, too whatever. Guess what? These are all lies we tell ourselves to keep us safe. Instinctually, we are designed to avoid situations that scare us or make us feel uncomfortable (and we think we have nailed evolution). Hundreds of years ago, we needed to pay attention to these instincts to keep us alive. This day and age, most of us do not need to worry about being eaten by a lion, but that ancient survival mechanism that our evolved selves have not yet shed switches into full gear to protect us from the proverbial lion. That lion could be the gorgeous man at the other side of the bar, a networking event that you thought you would attend alone, or an interview for a new job. Whatever *your* lion may be, remember this: fear and excitement have the same internal reaction. Both emotions are based on preconceived expectations that our brains have essentially made up. There is a reason F.E.A.R. stands for *false evidence appearing real*. Our inner voice tells us it's too scary out there, we could die if we quit our job, leave our unhealthy relationship, or go talk to that attractive man across the bar. So we end up living a dull, safe life in which nothing bad ever happens. Unfortunately, this also means nothing exciting ever happens. You decide. Do you listen to the bullshit you tell yourself to stay safe and live by the standards that society has deemed appropriate for your age and circumstance? Or do you step out, step up, and live big? Change your perspective on fear to see it as excitement. Chase your dreams, no matter if you are nineteen or ninety-one years of age. Do not die before you are dead, and do not let anyone but you decide how you live your life.

What do I hope you take away from this? I hope my story and my outlook will encourage you to find your truth and your happiness. Do not let anything or anyone, especially your age, limit you from exploring who you are or who you want to be.

As for me, I don't pretend to have all the answers. I don't see an end to this journey. It is an everyday, sometimes messy, sometimes hard, but mostly amazing adventure in the exploration of who I am. I continue to search for the things that make me happiest while spreading my passion and knowledge to anyone who will listen.

But I still have days when I question everything.

Am I doing this all wrong? Am I a fraud? Am I out here giving terrible advice? Who cares what I have to say? Maybe I fucked up.

Then I check in.

Am I coming from a place of love? Yes.

Am I happy? Yes.

Be brave. Be bold. Be truthful. Go out into the world and learn as much as you can, give back, and love with everything you have, because in the end, that is all that matters. Keep circling the sun being the best version of you. The world is waiting.

~ For my dad.

Timeless Practice:

◇— Repeat after me: It is never too early, it is never too late. —◇

◇———— Repeat again. ————◇

◇———— Repeat again. ————◇

CHAPTER 7

Time Is On Your Side

BY DEIRDRE SLATTERY

"Every day is chance to start new with
a clean slate; what will you map out for
your story starting now?"

~ Deirdre Slattery

Deirdre Slattery

www.deirdreslattery.arbonne.com

ig: deirdre_sfitness

fb: Deirdre Slattery - Fitness and Health Transformation Coach

. . . .

DEIRDRE SLATTERY IS A SINGLE MOTHER OF A BEAUTIFUL daughter who has brought out her passion for being a healthy, positive, and strong independent woman. She is always smiling and making the best of life around her. She is an eternal optimist with a grounded and practical balance. Seeing the best in people and their potential comes naturally to Deirdre. This free spirit has spent time travelling the globe and learning about life and feels especially at home near water and with people living healthy, thriving, and being happy. Her love for health and nutrition led her to pursue a second career as an entrepreneur in health, wellness, and fitness. Finding the good in every situation is what makes her life work meaningful. Her purpose is to spark hope and motivate others to stay positive and strong in the face of any adversity.

Deirdre received a Bachelor of Kinesiology and Education at the University of Windsor majoring in biology and health education. After twenty years, she is currently following her heart to expand her career in educating, training, and coaching others to live healthy and happy by sharing tools to become their best version of themselves. Nutrition, exercise, and a healthy mindset form the foundations of her healthy lifestyle. She derives the utmost fulfillment from helping others unlock and overcome their barriers to live the life of their dreams. Deidre is open-minded, kind-hearted, and always there to listen and guide others to their best life.

WHY DOES TIME PASS MORE QUICKLY THE OLDER WE GET? We spend our childhoods under the trees, watching the clouds move slowly, feeling as though life is endless and infinite, until without warning, time begins to move in a hurry. The summer comes to an end too quickly, and the cycle begins again with the school year, the sports seasons, the holiday season. All the while, we long for the weekend to pass more slowly and the vacations to last a bit longer, wishing and hoping we could pause time, even if just for a moment. We are always living in a state of being rushed, trying our best to complete all the tasks we feel obligated to do as adults and having nostalgia for what has passed.

How am I already here? I've asked myself this question many times. I feel like just yesterday, I was a carefree kid, and now I'm an adult, which seems much different than I expected it to be. I've wished for a chance to go back — to taste and smell and feel those moments that I remember, whether accurately or not, as wonderful.

How much of our time is spent living in the past and fantasizing about what could have been? How much time are we losing to regret or fear, instead of walking as confidently as we can? We can't change the past, just as we can't rush into the future, but we can choose to live in the now — putting our fear aside and instead pouring our energy into making good choices, taking action where we can, and setting up the best possible course for now.

I spent many sleepless nights in my early thirties, dreaming of a life I wished I was living. These hopes and dreams and, honestly, fears related to my career goals and aspirations. I'd had my daughter at this point, and I believe that being a parent brought a heightened awareness to the idea of time — as I focused on the weeks, months, and milestones in my daughter's life, my own life felt like it was going faster. I had this notion that it was too late to live the life I had dreamed of for myself; at the time, I really believed that. I would lie awake imagining the kind of businesses I wanted to launch and the dream jobs I wanted to pursue, while simultaneously grieving the loss of what I thought life would be like.

I was brave enough to share some of these desires with a very close friend, and he assured me I was not too old to go for it. But the story I kept telling myself was that it was way too late, I was too old, and I didn't have any professional training or experience to do what was in my heart. I felt hopeless about actually making a change. I would classify this time in my life as a sort of premature mid-life crisis. The what-if's largely consumed my mind. In hindsight, here's the lesson I learned: I needed to get out of my head and start moving toward my dreams with inspired action.

If you have any insecurities and doubts about not having enough or being enough, take action! It builds momentum and boosts your self-confidence. Teach yourself, take a course, find mentors and teachers, and jump in to what your heart wishes. It's never too late! Don't worry about whether or not it will work out, or about what people might say. Just start chipping away at what you want, and something good will come of it.

Unfortunately, instead of taking action right away, I put these ideas to bed for quite some time. Life, as they say, got in the way. I was trying to be a responsible adult and parent, working toward job security, pension, salary, benefits, retirement dates, all things that society was telling me I needed above all else. This kept me locked down, working toward an endpoint that felt increasingly less satisfying but that had zero risk involved. But I still had a nagging in my heart and soul that there was something more out there for me. That I could be a responsible parent and still do something I enjoyed doing! I always wanted to do something that would fulfill my sense of entrepreneurship and creativity.

Fast-forward to my late thirties, when life was more hectic than ever — I was running my daughter to school, racing to work, rushing to pick her up, getting dinner made, doing dishes, homework, bath time . . . I seemed to be in a contin-ual race that left me tired, stressed, and feeling like there was never enough time to simply enjoy life. Holidays and birthdays would come and go, making me feel overwhelmed and even more aware of how fast life was happening. I didn't even have time to daydream about what I wanted to do anymore, let alone do it!

Around this time, I had some difficult events transpire in my life that affected me deeply, and I spent many days feeling depressed, fearful, and sad. I didn't know where to go, what to do, or who to turn to; it felt like my life had been turned upside-down and shaken out.

It took until my fortieth birthday, and three more after that, for me to realize it was my responsibility to make my life happen in a way that was meaningful and that made me happy. If it was going to be, it was most definitely up to me, not anyone else.

I made the decision to take on new challenges and turn my frustrations, disap-pointment, and heartache into something positive for me. To start living a life in which I was happy, healthy, and in control. I created a massive shift in my life. I went from feeling powerless and thinking that half of my life was over to feeling empowered and purposeful, realizing that I still have the rest of my life to live. I decided to live it on purpose by partaking in meaningful experiences each day.

I paused my professional career of twenty years to become my own boss and discover what I am made of.

This was a journey. I went back to school to take some courses. I struggled, even failed at times, but I kept going. I needed to retrain my brain, lower my stress levels, and learn how to be a student again. Some people suggested that I might be making a mistake and that maybe this wasn't the right route to take, but I kept going. Enrolling in courses led me to meet new people and find new opportunities. I also decided to focus on my health and physical training so I could have more energy, lower my stress levels, and hopefully achieve more success, both mentally and physically. I hired a personal trainer and promised myself I would get in the best shape I could. From this action, I eventually landed a spot in a shoot for a fitness magazine — a dream come true and a testimony to how all my dedication, sacrifice, hard work, and action continued to have a ripple effect in my life.

At this point, I decided to recertify as a personal trainer and begin my own business. It took a great deal of courage to walk away from a salaried position with job and pension security, but it is the best decision I've ever made. Watching my clients grow and learn and become stronger encourages me every day. Being able to set my own schedule so that I can live a balanced life brings a joy of its own. By launching my business, I now have space in my schedule to prioritize what is truly important to me: spending time with my daughter. We get to truly enjoy each other's presence and build memories every moment, which is my personal definition of being a responsible adult and parent. I now ensure that I make every moment count.

As I age, my modeling career has continued to grow, which is the opposite of traditional modeling in which you have to be the youngest to get the opportunities. I am defying ageism by becoming healthier and happier as time passes. I feel and look youthful because I *am* youthful; that is my personality! Age is simply a number.

Being happy in our current life situation plays an important part in slowing down time. If you are stressing on Sunday about Monday morning, watching the clock or checking the calendar to get through the day or the job, waiting for Friday to arrive, then maybe it's time for a change — no matter your age, your income, your relationship status, or your location. When we start filling our days with what we love, time seems to become more meaningful and tangible, and the passing of time seems less threatening.

If you could create a perfect day for yourself, what would you do? If your ideal career was possible, would your level of happiness increase drastically? Take a chance on yourself! Pursue your true calling and discover your life's purpose, no matter your age.

Many successful people started out in a career much different than the one they eventually chose to make them happy and successful. Walt Disney was a newspaper editor for years before he was fired and eventually went on to build his empire and legacy. Martha Stewart was a model, stockbroker, and mother before she found her love of gourmet cooking. Jeff Bezos, founder of Amazon. com, was an investment banker before he took a chance on himself and launched his website from his garage. It's never too late to make a positive shift that might change your life!

I recommend writing out, in detail, all your greatest wishes and dreams for both your personal and your professional life. There is a statistically significant link between writing down aspirations and achieving them. Map out the life that you truly desire. Visualize yourself being in that life. Trust that you can make a change. When you decide what you truly want in your life, begin to take steps toward that big, audacious goal.

It can be overwhelming to imagine moving toward a goal that seems big and far away, especially if it's in a field or area of life you aren't currently familiar with. Remember that you can only do one thing at a time, and not everything has to be huge! It's about taking small steps that will accumulate into a bigger future. Be kind to yourself. Rome wasn't built in a day, but it was built by taking consistent action daily! Some examples of small steps toward a new goal might include:

Doing your research. Look into your desired career field, hobby, place to travel, etc.

- Begin to familiarize yourself with what this thing actually is, rather than what you imagine it will be in your head.

- When you are doing online research or reading books, newspapers, or journal articles, try to determine the realistic demands of pursuing this dream. Necessary prerequisites, whether in education or experience in the field? Cost? Timeline to achieve these goals?

- Write these things down so you can refer back to them throughout your journey.

Speak to some people who are knowledgeable about your area of interest. You might know someone who works in the field / has taken part in the hobby / travelled to where you want to go, etc. And if you do not know anyone, ask your network to connect you with someone. Remember that people enjoy sharing what they know, so don't be afraid to ask! The worst thing that will happen is they will say no, and you can move on to someone else!

- Make sure to ask whether there is anything important they have learned along the way that might be beneficial for you to know as you begin.

- Ask them for tips and tricks of the trade.

Say yes to opportunities that arise!

- Don't forget that it's one thing to want to do something and another to say yes when asked!

- Don't be afraid to jump into opportunities! Keep in mind that everyone has to start somewhere

- You don't have to be the best; you just need to do and begin to learn.

Here are some tips and tools you can use to help yourself refocus whenever you feel like time seems to be racing by.

Practice daily meditation for even a few minutes, followed by free and unfiltered journaling. This practice can reground you in the present moment, slow your brain, refocus your priorities, and clarify what you want and don't want. It can also help you to enjoy each moment more fully and remember what you are grateful for.

Move your body. Practicing yoga or any exercise you enjoy can help your mind focus on the current moment and help to slow your life.

Add more play and creativity in your life, however you can fit it in. Scheduling downtime for play, creativity, and unplugged time can make your life feel more full and meaningful.

Set small, achievable goals and tasks each day that help you create your dream life brick by brick. Small, consistent actions daily build momentum and confidence and ensure that you are living in the moment and taking messy yet inspired action. Action will leave you feeling accomplished, satisfied, and ready to do more! And when those goals are met, you already have a plan and vision for where you are going next.

My journey continues, and I am grateful that I'm taking action now and enjoying every day. Believe me, it is never too late to act on your goals and make those dreams a reality. By working toward my goals every single day and furthering my career, I can help my clients strive for better health and more energy and confidence to work away at their own goals. I try to slow time down by focusing on the things I'm grateful for and not worrying about the past or the future. Some days are still hard, sometimes I fall or fail, but I keep going. My hope is that you will find the courage to move toward your dreams. That if you fall, you'll get back up; if you are uncertain of where to go, you'll at least take the first step somewhere and trust the process, knowing that there is always time and space to redirect your steps and try again. The right people and opportunities will come your way as long as you continue to take action. I don't know what will happen tomorrow, and that's okay because I'm living in today, and today is a good day.

~ *When we listen for our calling and hear the voice within, we feel the desire for change. It is the courage to act on it, no matter the timing of our life or the circumstances; we can change our surroundings and circumstances to align with what truly makes us happy. I am fortunate to have a strong circle of support and a team of people for whom I am truly grateful who encourage me, especially during the more challenging moments, and believe in me, my life goals, and dreams. At the front of that line is my resilient and strong daughter, Lily, who is my heart and my "why" for going after my dreams and never quitting, but continuing to level up and build from where I am.*

CHAPTER 8

Life, Not According To Plan

BY SARA GUSTAFSON

"When we're obsessed with the life we're 'supposed' to be living, we miss out on the life we actually have."

~ Sara Gustafson

Sara Gustafson

ig: @light_love_words

fb: LightLoveWords

medium.com: @gustsa01

. . . .

SARA GUSTAFSON IS A WRITER AND EDITOR, GRAMMAR NERD, dog lover, and recovering perfectionist. She believes deeply in love, compassion, and the Oxford comma. One of her single greatest joys in life comes from helping other people tell their story, and tell it well.

Thanks to her teacher mother, Sara grew up surrounded by books and became fascinated by words and stories from a young age. Her interest in people's stories led her to major in history at Gettysburg College and to pursue a career in communications. She has written and edited for a wide range of industries, including international non-profit, real estate, biotech, construction and architecture, and health and wellness. Born and raised in central Massachusetts, Sara has lived in seven US states and overseas in South Korea. She now lives in Japan.

On my thirtieth birthday, I woke at daybreak in Vietnam. My husband and I drank cup after cup of strong Vietnamese coffee and ate bowls of dragon fruit as we gazed across an endless vista of green rice paddies. That afternoon, we strolled through a silk market and got caught in a sudden downpour, laughing as we ducked into a bar to dry out over cheap beers. Several days later, we hiked through the jungle, camping out under a full moon in one of the largest caves in the world.

Never in my life would I have imagined turning thirty in such a way.

My father experienced a much different Vietnam. In his early twenties, he was drafted into the United States Army and shipped overseas to fight in the Vietnam War. He spent his time in the jungle trying not to get shot.

Neither my father nor I expected to end up in Vietnam in any capacity. Camping in a Vietnamese cave was never anywhere in my life plan, and war was certainly not in my father's. So how did we end up there?

Buying Into "The Plan"

Growing up, many of us expect our lives to follow a certain timeline. Graduate high school. Go to a good college. Get a good job. Meet "the one" and settle down. Buy a house. Have kids. Move steadily up the career ladder and retire at age sixty-five.

Journal Prompt 1

Draw a timeline of the way your life was "supposed" to go, the way you imagined it as a child. Fill in all the big life milestones you dreamed of and when you wanted them to happen.

It's very easy to point the finger at society for our reliance on this timeline, and to a certain extent, I think that's true. All of us, men and women alike, face tremendous societal pressure to follow the crowd and do what we're "supposed", how we're "supposed" to be doing it. Conventional equals safe.

As humans, we also rely on a certain amount of predictability to help us make sense of the chaos that is life. Predictable also equals safe. I think that for most of us, looking forward into an empty void of a future would be paralyzing, which is why we plot our entire lives out into easily digestible chunks, convincing ourselves that by having a plan, we have control. The problem is, that's a lie. And when we start to realize that it's a lie — well, that's when the trouble starts for a lot of us.

When It All Falls Down

If your life plan has you scheduled to be married at age twenty-five, what happens when you find yourself still single at thirty? If you imagined yourself owning a single family home with a white picket fence by the time you're thirty years old, what happens when you can't afford that dream house? If a corner office was on your horizon by forty, what happens when your company undergoes a round of layoffs and you need to start from scratch?

What do we do then? How do we cope?

My life plan first fell apart after college, when I reached the "get a good job" portion of the story. I graduated with a degree in history, and no clue what I wanted to do with it. I chose to move in with my boyfriend and follow him around the country as he started his military career. In Florida, I worked at a Christian pre-school. In San Diego, I worked at a travel nurse recruiting agency and a technical publishing company. In New York, it was back to kids, this time at a daycare. I certainly wasn't building a career or finding my passion. I was floating, hoping that someday, it would come together and I'd be back on track.

According to my timeline, marriage should have come next. But a break-up came instead of an engagement — the second unraveling. The split had been looming over us for a while; we were good friends, comfortable, but nothing more. For months, we played a game of chicken in reverse, waiting to see who would be brave enough to call it off first. In the end, it was him.

I felt lost. I'd spent almost four years with him behind the wheel, using his career and his life as a way to mask the fact that my life was not going according to schedule. Now I had no choice but to face it. I moved to Washington, D.C. with a total of $400 in my bank account, took a job with an international non-profit organization, and met the man who would become my husband. Things finally seemed to be getting back to some sort of recognizable track.

Then my future husband got a job offer that he couldn't refuse — in Geoje, South Korea. I had never planned, or ever wanted, to live abroad. I had certainly never planned to live in a small fishing village on a tiny island in Asia. But that was the choice life presented me — start a new adventure with the man I loved or stay behind and try to follow the predictable path I was searching for.

I chose adventure and Korea. We discovered that it would be easier for me to get a visa if we were married, and after a month-long engagement, we had a tiny civil ceremony in my hometown in Massachusetts. In yet another instance of reality not aligning with what I'd always thought was "supposed" to happen, our Justice of the Peace's office turned out to be in his family's t-shirt and trophy shop. We exchanged vows in front of a trophy case filled with Ted Williams paraphernalia (rather fitting, looking back, for a lifelong Red Sox fan).

When many of my friends were buying homes and talking about starting families, I found myself putting most of my belongings in storage, packing a few suitcases, and leaving everything I knew. My life was going plan-less, once again. But this time, it felt free.

Saying Goodbye To "The Plan"

So how *do* we cope with a life plan gone awry? In my opinion, the first thing we need to do is face the cold, hard facts. The plan was always an illusion. We never had control.

The next step is leaning into that fact. When you learn to drive in the snow, they teach you to "steer into the skid." This means if you find yourself skidding out of control when you hit a patch of ice, don't try to correct it by steering the car back to where you want it to go. That will only make you skid more. Instead, turn the wheel in the direction the ice is taking your rear tires. This will help you recover from the skid and avoid a crash.

It might not be the most poetic thing to compare life to an out-of-control car on a patch of ice, but the metaphor speaks to my New England-raised heart. We cannot, by sheer force of will, direct the entire course of our lives. Sometimes we will hit a patch of ice and find ourselves facing a completely unexpected direction and as much as we'd like it to, fighting the skid won't help. We'll only make things harder on ourselves.

Journal Prompt 2

How have you been fighting life, trying to make it fit into your timeline? How would it feel to let go of that fight? What's the worst that might happen? What's the best?

The final step is finding joy in whatever — or sometimes despite whatever — life brings you. In college, I once interviewed my father about his time in Vietnam. My final question was, "What do you think was the biggest thing you took away from your experience?" His response rocks me to my core to this day.

In his quiet, simple way, he said, "All the things we complain about — annoying coworkers, fights with our spouse, not sleeping because of the baby, paying bills. A lot of guys over there never got to experience those things."

When I find myself bemoaning the fact that my life is not, and never will be, following a plan, I think about that quiet wisdom. What it boils down to is appreciating and being grateful for the stage you're in — even if you don't love it, even if it's not where you want to be. Find a way to appreciate it in some small way. Because this is your one life. If you're fixated on the "ideal" life you expected to live, you'll miss the one you actually have.

And I'm willing to bet that the life you actually have has included some pretty incredible experiences that you would never have planned. I never expected to live in Asia. I never dreamed I would be exploring Vietnam on my thirtieth birthday. I certainly never planned to get married in a trophy shop. But all of those things have been the absolute best parts of my life.

Journal Prompt 3

Look back at the timeline of your "perfect life." Now think of five positive things that you would never have experienced or lessons that you would never have learned if everything had gone according to plan.

When we try to plan out every milestone, we put ourselves in a box and limit the incredible things that can take place in our lives. We leave no for surprises, plot twists, growth — for life. We may let amazing opportunities pass us by because they don't fit in with what we think we should be doing. We may get complacent and not challenge ourselves and thus never know what we're truly capable of. We may hang on to jobs, relationships, and other life situations that have long since expired simply because they "look right." This is playing small, and it's no way to live.

Once I accepted the fact that life does not operate on my timeline, I started focusing less on *what* I wanted to experience in my life and more on *how* I want to experience my life. I want to approach life with a sense of curiosity. I want to embrace new experiences and opportunities and challenges with an open heart. I want to be filled with gratitude for what I have been given in my life, not resentment over what I have not.

This certainly doesn't mean that I've stopped setting goals or working to achieve them; what's changed is *how* I approach these goals. My view of my worth and of my life's worth is no longer tied to whether I achieve a certain milestone by a certain date. With this perspective, I find it easier to roll with the punches and adjust course when necessary. I've become less attached to the idea that my life needs to look a certain way in order to be fulfilling and happy. In turn, the process of pursuing my goals has become a lot lighter, a lot more fun, because I'm less attached to the outcome. I've also stretched way beyond my old comfort zones and learned that I am far more capable than I used to believe. This has made it easier to set and pursue newer, even bigger goals.

I know with absolute certainty that life is not finished throwing me curveballs. I know that many of them will be painful and hard. I also know that many will bring me experiences, people, and lessons that I never dreamed I needed. In fact, since I wrote the first draft of this chapter, we learned that my husband's job is once again taking us to Asia (this time, to Japan). We may not be able to choose the path that life carves out for us. But what we do have control over is *how* we react to where we find ourselves. We can react with resentment, anger, and fear when things don't go according to our plan. Or we can choose to loosen our grip, appreciate the things that we do have, and steer into our lives.

In the end, it's up to you — how do you want to experience your one life?

~ To Tom — thanks for the adventure of a lifetime.

SECTION 3

FEAR IS A TIME ROBBER

"Some people spend a lifetime in fear,
without ever knowing it."

~ Ky-Lee Hanson

FEATURING

Effie Mitskopoulos

Diana Zurbuchen

Tina Kalogrias

Yomi Marcus

Chapter 9

Is My Mind Playing Tricks On Me?

BY EFFIE MITSKOPOULOS

"Mold time to suit your needs and
manifest what you want!"

~ Effie Mitskopoulos

Effie Mitskopoulos

www.soulbodyhealer.com

e: soulbodyhealer@gmail.com | fb: soulbodyhealer

EFFIE MITSKOPOULOS, FOUNDER OF SOUL BODY HEALER, Is a registered social worker specializing in holistic psychotherapy. She combines customized Western interventions with hypnosis, mindfulness, yoga, and energy work. Her commitment to helping others stems from her own healing journey. Despite the hardships she faced, she kept receiving messages that there was more to life than suffering. Many times she felt like giving up, but hope and persistence kept her seeking knowledge, authenticity, spirituality, and ultimately, wellness. Her journey was catapulted in 2010 by practicing Kundalini yoga and becoming a yoga teacher. She came to realize that healing occurs on all levels: mind, body, and soul. Because much discomfort stems from a mental-emotional-energetic cause, practicing mindfulness and hypnosis shifts unconscious programs, thus aiding in management of emotional states, while Reiki and yoga bring balance and strength to the body and energetic systems by releasing unresolved emotions and energy blockages.

Effie has helped thousands of people through her programs on stress management, depression, anxiety, chronic pain, addiction, and trauma. She believes that every individual has special gifts and the strength to heal themselves. She is passionate about helping her clients uncover the root cause of their discomfort and release distressing patterns so they live happy, peaceful, and meaningful lives. Her vision is the uplifting of humanity — for people to feel whole, well, and free to express themselves fully so that every interaction is loving and compassionate, supporting a peaceful world.

IT MAY SEEM AS THOUGH TIME IS A CONSTANT FLOWING ENTITY. We use the clock to tell us when to wake up, when to eat, when to arrive at work, all the way throughout the day until we go to bed "on time." Often, I hear people telling me that they don't have enough time. I even catch myself thinking, *Where did the day go? I didn't get everything done that I needed to!* We seem to be a slave to time, time-starved! But isn't having more time just about being able to do the things you want or need to do? Isn't it all about experiencing what you really want to experience? Aren't we saying that we want to create space in our lives to spend and enjoy time with the people we love? The space to cook healthy meals to fuel our body, the time to do the activities that make us feel good, the time to go on vacation, the time in our schedule to even complete household chores because a tidy house means a tidy mind? What would it feel like if you could mold time to suit your needs so that you have enough of it and are manifesting what you want? Would that change your life? Just by changing your attention and perception, you can fill your schedule with things that bring you joy and still fit in your to-do list! Quantum physics shows us that everything emits specific patterns of energy and carries information, including our emotions, thoughts, attention, and perception.[5] For instance, when you're in a calm and peaceful state, this energy radiates outward and can affect the people around you. The theory of relativity says that time is relative to our energy and that space and time are a part of the same thing. Thus, how we think about things (a pattern of energy) affects our experience of time and what we manifest into our lives. For instance, if you feel anxious about being late for work and focus on that fear, you probably will be late. So why not let it go, put yourself in a calm state, and believe that you will arrive at work on time? This way, you are a co-creator of your experience and can mold space and time.

Attention And Perception: Time Travelling

You probably have experienced time in different ways; after all, it's all a matter of perception. Perhaps you have been completely engrossed watching a movie or having a conversation with your best friend — "Time flies when you're hav-

---

5   Dispenza, J. (2012). *Breaking the habit of being yourself*. New York, NY: Hay House Inc.

ing fun!" Perhaps you've been sitting around doing boring, remedial work and it seems to take forever — "A watched pot never boils!" In the first example, your attention is engulfed in the here and now, and you are experiencing enjoyment. In the second, your mind may be wandering to all the other things you could be doing instead of that boring work! Time has nothing to do with quantity and everything to do with attention and perception. When we are not focused on the task at hand, it takes longer to do. A distracted mind wastes time. So *where* are our minds then? When I ask my clients to journal where their thoughts go during the day, they notice that they're either looking back at a past event or anticipating or planning a future event. When you think of another time period, emotions from that time are triggered. These emotions produce chemicals that then secrete from your brain and into your body, creating a physiological effect as if that event were actually happening now. You have just time traveled.

This takes up time you currently have. It's easy to get distracted by thoughts, emotions, emails, phone notifications, etc. Then it takes twenty-five minutes to re-focus on what you were doing, and voila, you are running out of time!6 When we continue to think about another time period, the same emotions are continuously brought up and memorized, and it eventually becomes an automatic reaction. Then the same experiences keep recurring in our lives because we are stuck with auto-matic responses from that time period. Essentially, we end up living in that time.

Living In The Past

Think about something in the past — pleasant or unpleasant. Maybe it's when you got married; this could bring up pleasant emotions but it still takes up our time. We can create distress in this very moment as well, which takes up even more time. I was diagnosed with major depression when I was seventeen years old, and it lasted for ten years until I stopped living in the past. I remember my mind constantly unearthing old experiences — being rejected by peers, being reprimanded by my parents, or some other trauma. I continuously time travelled to these memories, thus bringing up feelings of unworthiness, inadequacy, sad-ness, guilt, hopelessness, etc. My brain memorized these emotions and turned them into depression. Bringing depression into my present generated an ex-pectation that my future would be more of the same. Perceiving the present with the same past (depressed) beliefs produced the same past thoughts and emotions. Because my energy (attention) was in the past, as the future unfold-ed, I remained stuck in the experience of depression. Now for the good news — anyone can get unstuck from any time period. At the age of thirty-four, I no

---

6   Mark, G., Gudith, D., & Klocke, U. (2008). *The Cost of Interrupted Work: More Speed and Stress.* Proceedings of the SIGCHI Conference on Human Factors in Computing Systems, Florence, Italy, April 5-10, 2008.

longer meet the criteria for depression. I haven't for several years now, partly because I got out of that past cycle of thinking and feeling, which opened me up to manifesting new experiences.

Living In The Future

When our minds focus on something that's not occurring now, our energy is somewhere else, which uses up the time we currently have. You could be thinking of things you need to do, daydreaming, or following whatever thoughts or images in your head that are not oriented to your task at hand. If our thoughts are distressing, those emotions slow us down even more. *Anxiety is the story of fearing a possible future.* It's when the mind says, "What if (this catastrophic thing) happens? What if I am rejected? What if I left the stove on? I have to do everything on my (long) list." Then both the brain and the body secrete chemicals as if that catastrophe actually is occurring in real time. But maybe you haven't spoken to that peer group yet, or maybe you did leave the stove on but the house didn't burn down. You also don't have to accomplish everything on your list!

The brain functions to keep us safe. It continuously monitors the environment for danger, hence keeping us stuck in a cycle of fear and anticipation in order to keep us safe day in and day out. However, it also keeps you in the future, where the problem hasn't even happened yet! So why focus on something you can't solve in this moment or on something that hasn't yet occurred? The mind also likes to overgeneralize, fearing an event will happen again, and focusing on it brings that feared future into our present life. For instance, you are frequently late for meetings; as a result, you begin anticipating you will be late, therefore fulfilling your own prophecy of being late over and over again. Focusing on the belief of "I am always late" tells the body that it's happening, which brings up emotions, such as anxiety, fear, disappointment, guilt, maybe even frustration, that we may feel when we think about being late. Then we think, act, and feel the same way we do when we actually are late. Furthermore, focusing on a feared event could bring up other emotions, and each emotion takes longer to process. For example, my being late provokes anxiety and guilt that the other person is waiting for me. The more stressful our thoughts and emotions are, the more they affect our brain and body on a cellular level and the longer it takes to do things. Not to mention, these emotions can leave us with poor sleep, fatigue, difficulty concentrating, etc., which slows us down even more. By worrying about a future that hasn't happened or will never happen, or by remembering a past that is already gone, we are not living in the present. Distress is probably not the experience you wish to manifest. Wouldn't it be nice if we had control over time travelling and the kind of experiences we bring into every moment we live in? We do — by employing a perspective beyond space and time, we are able to manifest any possibility!

Living In The Present: Manifesting Beyond Space And Time

How do you want to spend this moment? In the present, we communicate and maintain connected relationships, make decisions, pay bills, laugh, and everything else. When you're completely focused on experiencing something, feeling the emotions that surface and the sensations that arise, your intentions are being realized. Living from past experience or anticipating the future means you don't have the opportunity to have a novel experience; there is no new potential. This very moment is where you live greater than time because new experiences can happen. When we suspend judgments and future expectations, the present opens us up to all possibilities and we can create our heart's desires.

We must overcome the automatic reactions that make us time travel in order to fully be in the present moment. We can do this by applying mindfulness principles to the present experience. **Observe**, with your five senses, what is going on around you and within you. Be curious about it with a fresh mind, like a newborn baby. Everything babies see, feel, touch, smell, taste, and sense is new. Be an impartial researcher of your own experience.

Suspend judgment about your experience. It is the mind's nature to compare, judge, and evaluate; accept this fact. We judge things based on whether they are good or bad or whether they conform to our beliefs or philosophies. Our past experiences color our judgments, which may not reflect the current situation or our feelings accurately. In order to suspend judgment, we must observe the constant stream of judging and reacting that goes through our mind and decline to get caught up in it. Don't engage, follow, or reject it; just allow it to be as it is and then re-focus on the present.

Patience helps us understand that things are revealed in their own perfect timing. We need to give ourselves permission to allow an experience to happen, because we are having the experience anyway. Resistance, judgment, avoidance, or impatience do not take the experience away; rather, they make the experience persist by triggering further thoughts and emotions that keep it going. Remember, what you resist always persists. Just allow your experience to be, and then let it pass. Patience gives us space to gain wisdom from an experience and flow beyond time.

Accept the experience, no matter how painful, frightening, or undesirable it is; know that change, healing, and growth can occur. Acceptance is not about resigning or being passive; it is being *willing* to see things as they are. This removes extra emotions that take away from our productivity, thereby giving us time.

In our daily lives, we tend to DO everything for a reason and thus tend to expect certain results. Expectation doesn't create anything new. **Let go of any expectation** or striving for results in order to manifest the best possibility. Pay attention to what is happening, moment by moment. Make the intention to not attach to any thoughts, feelings, or situations — put them aside for the duration of your present experience or task. No need to speculate or attach an emotion to how something might go or how you might want it to go. Allow it to flow in its own time and be just as it is.

Set the intention to *be* in the present moment and **trust** that you are. Trust yourself, your feelings, and your intuition. Mindfully focusing on this very second, this very minute puts you in the flow, beyond space and time, where you can create any possible experience.

Living In The Flow: Play With Time

Time is perceived in different ways when we are in the flow. In hypnosis theory, we call this time distortion. When you've been watching an engaging movie and at the end, you can't believe two hours has gone by, you were beyond normal time and were in the flow. Time changed as your attention was engaged, your surroundings and body dissolved, and you became a consciousness (an awareness not bound by physical matter) observing the movie outside the flow of time. Our brains have this wonderful capacity to absorb a present moment and feel time and experiences differently. This is a meditative or hypnotic brain state. We drift in and out of this state throughout the day and go through it as we fall asleep and wake up. We can also operate from this restorative state with intention and affect our experiences in a powerful way. Our minds constantly create our reality based on the thoughts and beliefs we hold and on where we focus our attention.

We may have learned many limiting beliefs about time in childhood that have shaped our reality. We have been trained to perceive the world a certain way, so we can also retrain the mind to experience the world in a way that serves us better. We do this by changing our beliefs and focusing attention on what we want. It is possible to experience enough time. But belief does not come just by saying, "There is more than enough time for me" over and over again. We have to *feel* it in our body and *act differently*. Act and react differently so you experience a new feeling, i.e. you feel like you have enough time, are grateful for the time given, perhaps have a sense of calm and peace instead of feeling overwhelmed and frantically trying to get things done. Memorize this calm and then act this way when you have a lot on your agenda for the day. Secrete the emotions of what it's like to have more than enough time. Put yourself in that meditative state of mind to change the pattern so that your whole being believes you have more than enough time, and then you will!

The fun starts when we start experimenting. First, set the intention to bend time. Don't look at the clock for your entire ride to work; instead, believe you will get to work on time, even if you left your house later than usual. Visualize your punctuality, feel it in your body, meditate on it. Focusing and believing you will be on time results in the manifestation of it. Experiment with leaving yourself less time to do a task than you think you need. This will save you "analysis paralysis" time because work tends to fill the time that it's allotted (Parkinson's Law). For instance, if you have a whole day to do a certain task, it may take the whole day to do because you set no boundaries around it. It expanded to fill the entire day, with accompanying thoughts, emotions, and distractions, none of which you needed to finish the task and all of which made it take longer to complete.

Splitting our attention slows us down in the present. When our attention wanders, we can get stuck in other time periods, past or future, experiencing them over and over again. Then we create more of the same for ourselves: unpleasant experiences and not enough time. To live greater than time, we must overcome these automatic reactions by staying present; then we have access to all possible outcomes. In order to change time, and ultimately our experiences, we must focus on the present event without judgment and expectations and focus on being (thoughts and feelings) what we want. Now that you have a toolkit for how to conquer time, go have fun with it!

~ I thank Spirit for giving me the time and energy to manifest this chapter,
as well as all the loving people in my life.

CHAPTER 10

Time To Ditch Your Guilt And Your Fears

BY DIANA ZURBUCHEN

"When you get rid of any room for fear, your mindset and your heartset will clear up and open a path for amazing opportunities to find you."

~ Diana Zurbuchen

Diana Zurbuchen

www.dianazurbuchen.com

ig: missdeezee | fb: deezurbuchen

. . . .

A WEST COAST GIRL AT HEART, DIANA BREAKS AWAY FROM the often typecast military spouse. She currently resides in Calgary, Canada with her husband and their little rescue dog. Never one to let life's circumstances, no matter how unexpected or challenging, get in the way of her drive and determination to succeed, she brings her courage, passion, and open mind into all her endeavors.

Diana spent her childhood years freely hiking the mountains, spelunking the caves, and exploring the beaches of Vancouver Island. Her mom and dad, immigrants from Malaysia and Switzerland, respectively, have always taught her the importance of not getting held up by what others think and that where there is a will, there is a way.

Having earned her Bachelor of Commerce degree from the University of British Columbia, Diana works in corporate management and is a chartered professional in human resources by day. She has spent over fourteen years building her HR career; however, a few years ago, she stumbled upon a wonderful opportunity and fell in love with the ethics and the culture behind an incredible social marketing company. Diana has built a strong business alongside her thriving career, in which she has been able to flourish with confidence and hone her passion for personal growth, as well as uplift and empower others. She is the quintessence of altruism, known for helping a friend or a new acquaintance achieve their aspirations. Lively, amicable, and warm-hearted, Diana loves food, travel, and laughter. She most values the freedom of choice and being able to genuinely connect with people, both near and far.

"ΠƐШ ΥƐΛᖇ, ΠƐШ ᗰƐ" . . . "ΠƐШ ΥƐΛᖇ, ΠƐШ ᗰƐ." How often have we, at the start of a new year, a new month, or even a new day, told ourselves, "I can start my day new and win it *this* time! Today will be different! I won't procrastinate! I will not hit snooze and sleep in! I will make that call! I will close that deal! I won't be late for my meeting! I will get on top of my shit and not waste time!" Yet for some reason, as the day progresses, we end up regressing, feeling exhausted, defeated, as though we have lost all control of time, which keeps flying by quicker than we can run out to a Nordstrom shoe sale. Despite our best efforts, we somehow find ourselves ending up with more "to-do's" than time left at the end of the day. How defeating. How does this happen?

We all have that one friend who appears to be able to manage it all — juggling her successful career, her family life, her health and fitness, her home life, volunteer work, friends and social time. You name it, she does it. That friend who seems to always have a tidy home, a solid marriage, and her hair and brows on point and always exudes an aura as if she's perfectly put together and manages to accomplish it all with such grace? *You know who I'm talking about.* That one friend who is so productive, she magically can accomplish what most could not even fathom to do in a week, and somehow manages to compress it all within twenty-four hours while being completely functional on only five hours of sleep a night. *Who is she*?

Now, I have a confession to make. I think that person who sometimes pops into other people's minds is . . . ME. It only dawned on me when my friends started to comment about it, totally unprompted. *What? Shut the front door!* I seriously thought they had lost their mind or were just saying it to try to feed my ego on days when I melodramatically feel like I'm falling apart. *Is that seriously how some people see me?* In reality, this couldn't be further from the truth (at least in my mind, anyway).

The older I get and the more I rock my way into my thirties, I feel as though it's becoming progressively more challenging to balance it all. For the past few years, I have been feeling more like I'm thirty and tired, rather than thirty and thriving. Not sexy and definitely not how I expected to be rocking what should be my prime years.

From my experience — both socially or through my career and business — I find the two most frequently used excuses are: 1) I don't have enough money and 2) I don't have enough time. Nobody ever has enough time or money, regardless of our personal circumstances. Even if you are fortunate enough to have enough money, you certainly can't buy more time with that money. We all have the same twenty-four hours in a day. No more, no less, regardless of where you come from or your social demographic. How did we suddenly get to this place where we have to be and accomplish everything, and somehow have it all done yesterday?

I certainly know what it's like to feel as though I cannot get a handle on my time. However, from the many lessons I've learned through failing and getting myself back up more times than I care to count, I have become a firm believer that with some disciplined, daily commitment and an intentional purpose, it is possible to own your time rather than have time own you. Sounds so simple, right? I believe we can either work for time, or we can have time work for us and be on our side. What would you rather? I know without a doubt, I choose the latter.

In the summer of 2015, my husband's job in the military posted him to a small town called Wainwright. Population? 6,270 (well, maybe 6,268 now that we have moved away). I worked from home, but my career had me traveling very frequently. Life was grand considering our circumstances, and within a month after settling into my new surroundings, I got to work on my own business in the evenings and weekends like a total boss, alongside my incredibly busy career during the day. By the beginning of 2016, my little business had grown four-fold; by that fall, it had grown another 200 percent. I was incredibly excited for the growth but even happier with the fact that my business model gave me the ability to leverage my time, a concept I never truly understood until I embarked on the mystery world of entrepreneurship. Ironically though, after a few months of "handling it," I let myself slide when it came to making time for self-care. I was fully tapped out taking care of everyone and everything else. I didn't take the time to get a handle of my personal time and as a result, I felt like I was slowly falling apart from the inside out. Can anyone else relate?

This truly was the beginning of what would become the slow unraveling of any sense of control I had over my life, my time, and my health. While on the outside I seemed to have it all together, that couldn't have been further from the truth on the inside. I felt a strange and conflicting mix of exhausted, grateful, and unfulfilled. Talk about feeling like I had one foot pressed down on the accelerator and the other foot anchored on the brake.

In 2017, I decided to move back to the city and be long distance from my husband in order to seek some fulfillment and inspiration again. As if by physically going back to where I had once been happier, I would somehow magically make my internal shitstorm go away. I went back to work in a new job and within no time was off to the races, running at top speed again.

That summer, Ky-Lee Hanson, whom I had been introduced to by a mutual friend online, approached me with the opportunity to partner with this incredible and strong sisterhood of co-authors. I listened to the opportunity and immediately (but politely) declined. As exciting and wonderful as it sounded, my immediate reaction was, "What? I do not have time for this." I would be insane to even consider the possibility of taking on another project. I had a full-time job and was growing my business and volunteering on a very engaged Board of Directors, on top of juggling a family and married life, social life, fitness, health and wellness . . . insert every excuse possible here. Those clichéd excuses played through my mind like a broken record."I don't have the time, the capacity, or anything extra left in me to devote to another project," I said. Over and over again.

But despite the fears, I still had it tucked in the back of my mind — that tug at my heart, that curiosity, that little spark in me that whispered, *What if . . .?* I realized after a few months of excuses that I hadn't felt this excitement and curiosity since I jumped into starting my own social marketing business four years previously. Thinking back, that had been one of the best decisions I've ever made in my life. So what now? What have I got to lose? (Other than time, ironically).

Since that time, I feel as though my life has leveled up and has spun me around, upside down, backwards, and sideways. I have probably cried more times this year than I have in the past five years combined. In the span of a couple of months, I somehow listed two homes for sale in two different cities, sold one, rented out the other, bought a new home in a third city where we were relocating for my husband's career, had my car break down on me twice, purchased a new car, sold my old one, co-hosted a benefit fundraiser to support my friend in her fight against cancer, and negotiated an incredible job opportunity with a new company. Oh yes, all while I still worked my full-time job and tried to keep my business running. Phewf. *How in the world did I accomplish it and make it out alive?* Truth be told, most days were not pretty. Far from it. I had to put my head down and get to work.

The first and most important step was to remove the space that fear was occupying in my mind and in my heart. That *What if I fail / can't finish / make the wrong decision / suck / can't follow through / let others down / let myself down / don't achieve my target / run into too many roadblocks / run out of time / am not good enough?* noise does nothing but burn out your energy and waste what little precious time you do have. Trust me on that one. I have learned it the hard way, and I am honestly still working on removing the fear every single day. Some days I do well at it; other days are an absolute failure. As the Japanese proverb goes, *"Fall down seven times; get up eight."* I have learned countless times that when I am determined and remove the space for fear in my life, the end result is always some new, crazy opportunity, one that I have never even dreamed of. The space frees up so that you are able to complete everything you need to in the time that you have. It truly all falls into place the way it should, if only we create the space to let it.

So what happens when that sneaky snake named fear starts creeping in again? Whenever I start doubting myself, I think, *What kind of leader or example would I be to other women, boss babes, corporate professionals, or resilient and strong mamas out there (or even kids, if I had any!) if I didn't open up the space within me and let curiosity and opportunity in?* Telling ourselves that we are "busy" (I despise that four-letter word) does not serve anyone or anything but the mysterious abyss into which time seems to escape.

I have learned and tailored a simple yet incredibly effective tool for myself, taken from a coaching program I completed by Brandon Barber. This works great in both your personal and your professional life. Every morning, spend just a few minutes dedicated to writing out your daily "Four D's":

DO — What are **three** things (tops!) I must absolutely do today? I never write more than three. Some days they may be three big things. Other days when I'm overwhelmed, it might be something as ridiculous as "finish briefing note, work out, call three clients." To the best of my ability, I never go to bed without completing the top three of the day.

DUMP — What is truly not a priority for **me?** (*Note: taking care of your physical or mental health should never be on the "Dump" list.) List the things that are not a priority. Dump them and forget it! There is no point in letting them take up any more of your time or mind space. Some days, it might be a social event if I have to meet a deadline or take a personal day for myself. Most days, however, it's the many forms of media (TV, social media, mindless browsing, even the news) by which I can easily get distracted.

DATE — What do I need to do but doesn't have to happen right this instant? Date it in your calendar and schedule it in. What's important that can be scheduled for the near future? A vehicle service appointment? Clearing out your inbox? Sometimes, for me at least, it's scheduling in a date night with my husband by putting a placeholder in our respective Outlook calendars!

DELEGATE — What needs to get done but does not **have** to get done by me? Can someone else help me with this task (be it a spouse, administrative assistant, friend, someone to clean your house, someone to do your home repairs or renovations)? As successful women, it's common to feel like we need to do everything ourselves so that it is done "perfectly." However, this is not a need; rather, it is a *preference*, a way for us to exercise complete control in our lives, only to lose control over our time and energy because we are spread too thin. If someone else can do it 80 percent as well as you would yourself — delegate it. Life is about appreciating more joy, love, and growth instead of being fixated on perfecting all the tasks. This past year, I learned that I need to let go of the significance I place on certain tasks. As much as I love to cook, there have been some months in which I have ordered a food preparation service so I didn't have to end up cooking healthy dinners at 11:00pm every night. Some crazy weeks, it may be bringing our dog to daycare so he will get playtime and exercise while I tend to other matters, or even hiring someone to clean our home. Some months when fear has settled in me deeply, I've invested in an executive/personal coach to help me work on strengthening my mindset and beliefs so that I can be more effective with my time in achieving my goals. Those one hour, bi-weekly coaching sessions end up saving more time for me in the long run. My point is, utilize the resources around you and learn to let go of some of tasks so that you can leverage your time to be able to focus on other priorities, such as your health, your family, or your business.

My hope for you going forward is that you stop allowing guilt to set in about doing things that won't grow you or that don't align with your or your family's goals. Unless, of course, those ends will justify the means. Then by all means, work it like a boss! But remember, it won't be serving anyone in the long run if you're left feeling resentful and disgruntled by giving in to something that doesn't align for you. This is a work in progress that I have struggled with for decades, so I can only imagine that you may sometimes feel this way, too. Remember to trust yourself because you are incredibly capable and strong! Remove the space for fear in your mind and your heart. Allow the room for intrigue, inquiry, and opportunity to set in. As another great mentor and speaker, Keith Kochner, says, *"You cannot walk towards your greatness; you can only walk away from it."* You are an inspiration whose light is waiting to shine in greatness. So decide now, each and every day, to remove that space for fear and make space for things that energize your spirit, tug at your heartstrings, and pique your curiosity so that only greatness can come through. I can't wait to hear all about it and welcome you to share your wins with me, no matter how big or small!

I'm cheering you on!
With all my love and support,
xox Diana

~ My heart bursts with such gratitude, as my cup has been overflowing with so much encouragement, needed inspiration, and heart-centered, positive vibes from everyone I'm blessed to be surrounded by. To my husband, Marshall, for the tough love and encouragement when I start doubting myself. To my wonderful parents who love me endlessly and never miss a beat to check in on me, I love you and thank you. To my wonderful inner tribe of women and men I am so blessed to do business with, and without whom this amazing

opportunity would never have presented itself. To my friends and everyone else who has ever crossed my path, whether it be for an instant or an everlasting moment, you have all had an impact on me, I have learned so much just being around you and getting to know you. Thank you!

Chapter 11

Lost In The Depths
Of Time

BY Tina Kalogrias

"Time flies by and if we aren't careful,
our life can flash before us."

~ Tina Kalogrias

Tina Kalogrias

www.accentsandelements.com | www.annassawellness.com

ig: accentsandelements | annassawellness

. . . .

TINA KALOGRIAS IS AN ENTREPRENEUR, MOM, DAUGHTER, AND SISTER. Her first passion is her family: her loving and supportive husband and her beautiful daughter and handsome son. They will always be her purpose in life. She also has a passion for cooking and for telling a story with her interior design and home staging business, Accents & Elements.

While Tina loves her life, she was lost for a long time. Mindful meditation helped her find herself and discover her internal power through self-love, self-care, and self-awareness; she later became a certified meditation coach. Tina loves helping people find their inner peace and discover their passion and purpose through their own meditation practice. Recently, she started a website called Annassa Wellness, along with her partners, Ann Lombardos and Georgia Lombardos. She and her partners hope that this space can help empower other women to be in love with themselves and their lives. In Greek, Annassa means breath, and Tina chose this name because it resonated with her meditation practice.

Tina believes we are all here for a reason and we need to discover our passion. She hopes that her story helps inspire other women to look within and find their true selves and live a happier, more joyful life.

I WAS IN OUR FIFTH HOME WHEN ANOTHER SUDDEN PANIC ATTACK AROSE. This one was a doozy. I felt like I was drowning; the room spun and everything went dark, and all I could do was fall into my husband's arms.

This was the moment when I realized that I might be in trouble and that I had no choice but to take those antidepressants that our family doctor had prescribed. I hadn't taken them because I was ashamed of my "weakness" and I was in denial. I didn't want to admit to myself that I suffered from anxiety, suffered from a mental illness. But when I saw fears in the eyes of my husband, a fearless man, *that* was the turning point for me. I knew I had to do everything I could to fight this and get better.

All my life, I was told that when you leave the house you have to be perfect. You have to leave your problems at home, make sure no one knew your troubles, your fears, your secrets. I was taught to wear my mask well. I was led to believe the world was a big bad place where bad people lurked and everyone was out to hurt you. People are evil, they are jealous, they want what you have, and you can't show weakness or vulnerability. I grew up feeling like I couldn't trust anyone and I couldn't express my feelings. So the walls went up, and that's where they stayed, until that night.

The next day, I made the call to the therapist. I had seen psychologists before, but I guess, maybe, I hadn't actually confronted the core fears that haunted me still. Angela, my therapist, called it rage and said I couldn't connect to the pain and fear I felt.

I was born into a family business with a dominant father and a controlling mother. My parents doted on their son and treated their daughters like second-class citizens. That pain had caught up with me. I was miserable running my family's business and felt lost and devoid of any fulfillment underneath the facade of perfection. I had to be the perfect daughter, perfect sister, perfect wife, and perfect mother. I had to portray an image of success and compete with other women. I had to be the prettiest, the thinnest, and the richest.

I was physically, mentally, and emotionally exhausted! I had always worn a mask, but now I felt like the masquerade was over, my mask fallen and shattered. I could no longer pretend otherwise; my body and mind screamed for help.

I had let too much time go by, neglecting myself and the subtle messages my body was sending me. It was time to listen to those messages, take care of myself, and focus on my mental health.

"Believe in the promise of today, and have hope in the possibilities of tomorrow." ~ Chris Burkmenn

We constantly complain about how time flies and how busy we are. But are we busy? Are we so busy that we cannot make time for the present moment? Live in the moment — that is how you get time on your side. Does that mean we don't plan for tomorrow? Of course not! Plan and organize your tomorrow, but when you finish filling your agenda, make sure you come back to NOW.

Mindful living has become the new buzzword everywhere. I discovered the meaning of mindful living, or living in the now, because, in a way, I was forced to. My anxiety was wreaking havoc on my health. My panic attacks had me feeling like my tomorrow would never come. Fear limited me and kept me constantly living in tomorrow, and on the sidelines of my present life.

I had to learn to control my anxiety fast. My family doctor referred me to an osteopath, and she saved me. She suggested I meditate three times a day: before breakfast, before supper, and before bed. "Start with five to ten minutes," she said.

Mindful living helped me forget about tomorrow, and my time spent meditating became my today. When I focused on the now, I put myself in the present moment, which not only eliminated the fear of tomorrow but kept me from thinking about it. Mindful meditation helps us to live a fuller life. Life feels brighter, sounds are clearer, and the colors and details of the world around us become more apparent. For me, it's almost like stopping time and putting everything in slow motion. You don't stop doing things; you just start feeling them and living them.

All We Need To Do Is Bring More Awareness To The Things We Do

Take eating a meal. Often, we eat so quickly that we barely notice what we are putting in our mouths, or we eat in front of the television with our devices. Eating more mindfully just means that we bring an awareness to our food and how we eat it; savor the taste of your food, feel its texture, inhale its flavor and aroma. Tune into how you feel when you eat certain foods; doing so will satiate you more fully.

The same goes for life. If we slowed down and brought awareness to the present moment, we would experience it more, truly feel it instead of feeling like it was passing us by. John Kabbat-Zin said, *"The best way to capture moments is to pay attention. This is how we cultivate mindfulness."*

We think because we are stuck somewhere, like in a waiting room or in traffic, we are losing time. But if we stop and pay attention, take things in and be more mindful of our surroundings, and use the time we have, we can actually gain time.

"Light tomorrow, with today!" ~ Elizabeth Barrett Browning

I used to waste a lot of time worrying about the mistakes I made in the past. *What if I had done things differently?* Worrying about what happened yesterday or what will happen tomorrow is a waste of time, because living in the past leads to depression and living in the future leads to anxiety. So why not live in the present and find joy in the moment? Why not find joy and gratitude within the little everyday things that make up life itself?

Mindfulness has helped me make peace with time. I try not to fight it. I try and embrace time and put it on my side. Of course it takes practice; I have been practicing mindful meditation for two years now and it has created a different mindset and attitude about the concept of time. Focusing on breathing in my meditation practice has taught me how to bring myself into the present. Our thoughts will always try to bring us somewhere else other than here and now. But with breath control, I shift my attention to my chest and my heart, and remind myself to come back to now.

Make Time For Yourself

We all have so much to do! Take care of our children, our pets, our aging parents, work, and home, but what about taking care of ourselves?

When I was faced with my anxiety diagnosis, I realized that all I had to do to control it was make time for myself. Meditation teaches you to slow down and be compassionate and kind to yourself.

I used to work out regularly, but I had stopped for almost two years. I would tell myself that I had no time or that I needed to take care of my family first. As a result, I gained twenty-five pounds and felt exhausted, angry, and unhappy.

After my diagnosis, my New Year's resolution became making time for myself. I started working out again; I took two hours for myself and found myself in the process. I lost fifteen pounds, regained my energy, and found joy once again!

It wasn't the act of going to the gym that brought me joy and happiness; rather, it was the very conscious act of making time for myself. Time for yourself can come in many different forms. My joy came from small things, such as walking my dog, sitting on my porch, hugging my children, cooking a meal for my family, and focusing on what I had rather than what I didn't have. These things all made me feel immense gratitude; I was grateful to be making time for myself.

Do we have time for ourselves? Maybe we don't, but we have the power to make time. All we have to do is carve out a small moment. It doesn't have to be two hours; something as short as thirty minutes is just enough time to bring attention to our self and pause for a moment and breathe!

Slowing Down

Lately, all that's on my mind is, *Will I have enough time to do all the things I want to do?* This is a recent development because before this moment in my life, I didn't have such big goals!

Discovering my anxiety diagnosis was nothing compared to discovering the hole in my heart.

All of a sudden I felt my mortality! I had lived life as if I were a vampire, thinking I would live forever and had all the time in the world.

My anxiety turned out to be a blessing in disguise because I learned that we can actually control our fears by facing them head on and not avoiding them. I confided in an old friend about my anxiety and about how unhappy and unfulfilled I felt with my job and life. She admitted that she felt the same and in that moment, I felt relieved and hopeful. *That* was the moment I realized I wasn't alone. At least one other person felt like me, and that was comforting. I drew some weird sense of strength from that, and it launched me into a journey of self-discovery that hasn't stopped since.

For almost thirty years, I had been searching for something to define me, something to give me purpose. I didn't know what I wanted or why I felt lost and unhappy. In an odd way, if my anxiety and my panic attacks hadn't forced me to slow down and take time for myself, I would have never discovered myself, my passion, and who I am and what I wanted to do.

I started my interior design/home staging company, Accents & Elements, and my journey to joy hasn't stopped since. Practicing mindfulness and gratitude helped me discover my passion and my purpose. I feel the two go hand-in-hand because your passion brings you happiness and all of a sudden, you want to share that happiness with others. You become so much more in tune with yourself and how good it feels to be living out your purpose that you want to shout it out from a rooftop. *Look, you can be happy, too!*

After a workshop with Shannon Walsh, my life coach, my purpose suddenly became clear. I needed to share my story, share how I found my way out of an unhappy and unfulfilled life. Like Buddha said, *"Every experience. No matter how bad it seems. Holds within it a blessing of some kind. The goal is to find it."*

That's where Annassa Wellness online began. I wanted a place where I could share my experience with meditation and breathwork. I wanted to share what it meant to slow down and let go of our fears by facing them head on. In Greek, *Annassa* means breath. By bringing our awareness back to our breath, we can focus on the moment and be mindful of the present, thus cultivating more time in our day. By incorporating a daily practice of breathwork and meditation, we can discover our inner strengths and with this, we can discover who we are and our passion and purpose in life.

Living in the moment has helped me slow time down. It has helped put time on my side.

Love & light,

Tina Kalogrias

~ To my husband Tom, I thank you for all you have taught me, for believing in me, and helping me find my true self. To my children Dimitri and Anna-Angelika, for being my inspiration, my joy, and raison d'être. To my parents, thank you for your unconditional love. To Angelia Mantis, I would have never had the courage if you didn't believe I could. To Maddy, who said: you look like a boss woman, all you have to do is act like one. To Lisa and Stephane for mindfulness and meditation. To Ann and Georgia thank you for showing up when I was ready for you both. To life, you surprised me in my darkest moments by shining your light.

Timeless Practice:

◇— What are you scared of? Where —◇
does fear show up in your life
and prevent you from living
intentionally?

◈

◈

◈

◇— Are you ready to turn that fear —◇
into courage?

◈

◇— What daily actions will you take —◇
to understand and overcome
this fear?

◈

◈

◈

CHAPTER 12

The Wait Is Over . . .
Your Time Is Now!

BY YOMI MARCUS

"For years, you focused all your energy on keeping YOURSELF down, hiding who you are, and watching your life go by. Now you have two choices. You can keep waiting and watching, or you can end the wait and uncover the amazing person you are."

~ Yomi Marcus

Yomi Marcus

info@yomilifestyle.com

yomilifestyle.com

· · · · · · · · · · · ·

YOMI IS A HEALTH COACH WHO IS PASSIONATE ABOUT HELPING WOMEN reach their fitness goals, develop positive habits, and create a healthy lifestyle they love. She does this in her health programs and groups that address physical fitness, confidence, mindset, and food. Her goal is to hold space for women to fully embrace who they are while nurturing a healthy mind and body.

Since her elementary school days, Yomi loved creating and expressing herself using performance, words, and the arts. Yomi graduated from the University of Alberta with a degree in psychology. She later studied to become a certified teacher and then a fitness specialist and coach. Education became her passion, as she loved watching people learn and transform for the better. Yomi worked as a teacher while training and coaching women to their health goals. In 2013, she decided to begin her own fitness transformation and registered to compete in a fitness competition. Although the experience was challenging, Yomi placed first in her second competition, receiving her PRO card.

These days, Yomi is making Toronto home and is loving the experience. She enjoys meeting people, attending community events, and embarking on new adventures. According to Yomi, travelling and food are, by far, two of the best gifts to mankind. She also values self-discipline, self-care, and a happy, healthy lifestyle.

MANY OF US ARE PART OF THE "WAITING" CLASS — waiting for the right time, place, sign, or feeling before we take action and create change. The sad thing about the waiting class is that we will wait forever. The truth is, there is no such thing as the right time! The right place doesn't exist in the real world, and a great neon sign will not magically appear in front of us. That one thing that is "supposed" to happen to prove we are ready and to push us out of the waiting class is not going to happen.

Each year, tradition has us writing out resolutions or things we want to accomplish within the next twelve months. Health and fitness goals often top many of our New Year's resolution lists. How many people would love to lose weight, gain muscle, and feel amazing in their body? Yet every year, these resolutions quickly become broken promises that we put away on a shelf to gather dust as we continue on with life. The truth is, many of us will never accomplish our goal because we have put it in the waiting class — a quiet room of forgotten dreams, frustrations, limitations, and things that will simply never happen. The waiting class is our comfort zone. A few years ago, I made a change and a new health and fitness goal. I wanted to compete in a fitness competition. I had done nothing like it before. Was I ready for it? The answer was an emphatic, "No." My lifestyle and thought patterns all indicated that I was not ready to begin that journey and wouldn't be able to cope with the rigorous workout routine and discipline it required. I was an average woman who loved going to restaurants and often frequented well-known fast-food establishments. I lacked self-confidence and was extremely sensitive — I would literally have an internal panic attack when someone so much as looked at me funny.

In the weeks before meeting with my coach, my mind filled with thoughts like, *Are you sure you can do this? What if you fail? Are you sure you can measure up? Maybe you should wait for the right time. Maybe you should wait till you have more money . . .* I chose not to listen to those thoughts. The day I stood on stage with my first place medal, after months of exhausting 5am workout sessions, hours of cardio, and dietary restrictions, my happiness knew no bounds! My heart was racing and my mind was full of happy thoughts because I had accomplished what I had set out to do.

How did I do it? What happened between the fear and uncertainty on day one and the success and laughter on the day I won the competition? My journey can be summed up in eight steps that I believe can be used by anyone in pursuit of any dream or goal. But first, let's uncover why so many of us choose to spend so much time in the waiting class.

The Comfort Of The Waiting Class

Waiting is comfortable. Remaining the same *is comfortable*. Picture a quiet room full of soft pillows and warm blankets that say, "It's okay, just relax here. No rush." The teacher of the class spends his or her time asleep and leaves you unchallenged and unengaged. It may seem fun right now. You can do, or not do, as you wish. The problem with the waiting class is this: We stay there for years existing on autopilot with only a small suspicion that there is something more to life outside that small room. That small burning flame can show up in our lives as frustration, boredom, sadness, emptiness, pain, etc. We might have no idea where those feelings are coming from or why they start bubbling to the surface.

Sometimes we wake up from a mindless slumber and move into a state of self-awareness and want to get out of that waiting class. However, by that time, we might feel we have arrived at the party a little too late; we realize how far we could be had we awakened or started earlier, and we watch as others have progressed ahead of us.

No, this is not about comparing ourselves to others. It's about knowing that every single one of us possesses the power within ourselves to be successful, and we can take the action now!

I propose that the idea of "waiting for the right time" or "I'll start next week" to do something we desire is a perpetual lie we tell ourselves (and others) to make us feel better, when in fact, we have no intention of following through with it. And even if we do have an intention to start, we have no intention of committing to it. Waiting for the "right time" means limiting ourselves and dulling our greatness. It is telling God, Creator, Universe, and the world that we are not born as ready, powerful, worthy, capable beings. The result is a lifetime seat in the waiting class and constantly missing out on life's successes.

Breaking Out

Breaking out of the waiting class will take considerable effort. It is our comfort zone, we love it there, and our whole being is fighting against us to stay where it is safe and familiar.

Here are four obstacles that fight against us and keep us in the same spot . . . waiting:

1. Ingrained habits. "Habits" are actions we engage in on a regular basis that have become somewhat automatic patterns. We don't think about these things

— we just do them. Smoking, brushing our teeth, biting our fingernails, our eating routine, the way we sleep, and the way we exercise are all learned habits. Often, habits are formed as a way of preventing or creating an emotion. Smoking and fingernail biting, for example, may have begun as a way of preventing feelings of stress and anxiety. These habits fill us with a sense of calm, so we continue the behavior because they become the solution to our negative feelings. Our brains begin connecting the feeling of stress and anxiety to that activity or solution. We learn to quickly pick up a cigarette or bite a nail whenever we feel the onset of stress, anxiety, fear, loneliness, anger, etc. To get out of the waiting class, we must find a way to overcome our strong automated processes.

2. Limiting beliefs. What we truly believe about ourselves, others, and our world affects our ability to get out of the waiting class. Henry Ford summed this up perfectly by saying, *"Whether you think you can or you think you can't, you're right."* I saw my limiting beliefs at work in different parts of my fitness journey. In one instance, my stagecoach pulled me aside and stated, "There is something blocking you. I am not sure what it is." I didn't know what it was at the time either but it showed up as frustration, resistance, restraint. This was the belief that "I am not good enough," and it sucked my confidence and halted my freedom of expression.

In order to succeed and achieve the goals we set for ourselves, limiting beliefs have to be dealt with. Finding a way to take messy, massive, and inspired action despite those negative beliefs may be our biggest success story yet.

3. Perception of your history. The way we view our past can either break us down or build us up. If you take a moment to be honest with yourself and truly reflect on how you have used your time on the planet so far, what are some words that come up? Are they negative words like failure, useless, pathetic, broken, sucks, etc.? Or are they words of affirmation such as blessed, progress, learn, gratitude?

You can perceive time as your enemy (working against you, limiting you, taunting you, causing you to fail) or as your teacher (working with you, supporting you, teaching you, helping you to be exactly who you were meant to be).

4. Fear of the unknown. The best thing about waiting for the "right time" is that you get to stay in the comfort of the waiting class. It's easy there because we know it. We have spent so much time there that we know exactly what it looks like, smells like, feels like. We can move around the classroom with our eyes closed and never bump into anything. Outside the waiting class, however, lies the unknown, which is daunting and terrifying to explore. *If we venture out of that comfort zone, what will happen? What will people think? What if I don't succeed? What if he or she doesn't like me? What if I fail like I have done so many times in the past?* We often think these types of thoughts when starting something new. Change is not a comfortable process; after all, we have years and decades of automated patterns to overcome.

Neale Donald Walsch put it so simply: *"Life begins at the end of your comfort zone."* The only way to tap into our possibilities is to stop waiting and start doing!

The Transition

On the journey to your health and fitness goal (and quite frankly, any goal), a significant change must happen. We just talked about how much is stacked against us to ensure that we remain stagnant and safe in life. For this reason, we must undergo a mindset shift in order to prepare us for combat. And yes, it is definitely a battle. You have to want it!

The Eight Steps To Stop Waiting And Start Succeeding

I faced many challenges on my journey to the fitness stage, both physical challenges and changes (sore yet bigger and stronger muscles) and mental challenges and changes (self-doubt, frustrations, uncertainty, etc.). I can summarize how I overcame those challenges in eight steps that can help you get out of the waiting class and transition into a lifestyle of success:

1. **Acknowledge where you are and how you got there.** Have an honest, fact-based conversation with yourself about what brought you here. The goal is to take ownership and be accountable without blaming yourself or making yourself feel guilty for the decisions you have made or not made. We need to be completely authentic and transparent with ourselves

2. **Accept yourself and know you are worthy just the way you are.** Once you have acknowledged where you are and have taken responsibility for your situation, it's time to accept yourself as a lovable, worthy, and capable human being.

3. **Re-discover your *Why*.** Make sure you have a strong *Why* because *that* is what will propel you to spring into action. Chances are that you might notice your goals need to be re-evaluated and restructured to be more specific and more in-line with what you want in life.

4. **Visualize where you want to be.** Paint a picture in your mind. How does it feel? What are some textures you see and feel? Where are you at this moment? Imagine you have accomplished your goal — how do you feel, what do you see, and what do you do? We take a powerful stance when we can live in that visualization. The key here is to focus on the picture and how you want to feel, and to appreciate the journey needed to get there.

5. **Act "as if."** Another powerful step in embodying the person we want to be is by acting "as if" we are *that* person right now or, at the very least, acting "as if" we have the potential to be *that* person right now. This shift can spring us into action instantly! How powerful is it to see yourself as a fitness model now instead of someone *trying* to be a fitness model? Which person would be more likely to get up at 5am for a workout or to say '"no" to a burger and fries? The person who *is* a fitness model or the person who is simply *trying* to be one?

6. Get a support system or community. The people we allow into our lives and interact with regularly matter. Do they move us closer to our goal or further from it? The people and things that move us away from your goals have no business being part of your journey, at least not now. It's important to be cautious of the people we let influence us. We must find people who support us, hold us accountable, and allow us to grow. That is why I invested in a fitness coach (and still have other coaches today) and joined a community. When we choose to make a change and get out of waiting, we will need all the support we can get.

7. Decide. This might seem simple, but it can be the hardest step of all. The decision to act now instead of waiting for the "right time" needs to be a conscious one. Someone taught me that opting not to make a decision is a decision in itself. Not making a decision, or waiting to make a decision, is like telling ourselves we are not important or we do not deserve a live a life we love.

8. Commit to yourself. Commitment is one step above deciding. It's making that promise that we will act despite all else. It's acting even when we don't feel like it. It's going to the gym instead of a party, taking a rain-check on a pizza night invite, or staying up late to work on your business. After the excitement and glamor wears off, commitment keeps us loyal to the cause.

Take a moment, right now, in a quiet place and clear your mind of distraction. Now picture your goal, be it health-, career-, or life-related. See yourself accomplishing that goal. How does it feel? What do you see? What do you think? What are the types of things you do? Take yourself to that place and embody it. Fully embrace the experience as if it is happening right now!

Take a moment to write down the answers to these questions. Dig deep and describe every little thing in detail — how it feels, what you see, what you want, why you want it, and more.

Instead of living our days waiting for the right time, the right moment, a sign, let's use this moment as a teacher to unlock the possibilities we want to create for our lives.

Picture a life in which we do not wait to act on our dreams. A world in which procrastination and hesitation do not keep us from doing the things we want and need to do. Imagine a place where we do not make excuses for ourselves or validate our inaction. Imagine saying the things that need to be said when they *need* to be said and doing the things that need to be done exactly when they *need* to be done. Now go do them!

~ To my wonderful parents and brother: thank you for all of your love and support. Words can't express how grateful I am for all the wonderful experiences you have made possible. To my friend Amy: thank you for encouraging me to take the step and be part of this amazing compilation. I am looking forward to more coffee dates with you this year. I am internally grateful to Golden Brick Road Publishing House and Ky-Lee Hanson for this opportunity. Thank you for the positive experience. To the editing team, thank you for your amazing work and for bringing out the best in my words. To all my friends and family: thank you for being here.

SECTION 4

HEARTBEAT TO HEARTBEAT

"Time does NOT heal wounds,
progressive action does."

~ Ky-Lee Hanson

FEATURING

Stephanie Butler

Falon Joy Malec

Julie Chessell

Charleyne Oulton

CHAPTER 13

Change Your Timeline

BY STEPHANIE BUTLER

"One way to make every moment count
is to live from a grateful heart."

~ Stephanie Butler

Stephanie Butler

www.serenityorganizingsolutions.ca

fb: SerenityOrganizingSolutionswithStephanie

· · · · · · · · · · · ·

STEPHANIE WEARS MANY HATS; SHE IS A COMMUNITY HEALTH WORKER, a writer, and a professional organizer. She loves working with people in a helping capacity. Stephanie grew up in North Toronto but has moved further north to Barrie, where she enjoys the waterfront, hiking trails, and spending time with friends and family. In her free time, she enjoys crafting, travel, and relaxing with her two furbabies. Stephanie wrote in the first of the Dear Woman Series, *Dear Stress, I'm Breaking Up With You,* and is excited to be part of this volume. She hopes her life experiences will guide others to work through their own experiences and not feel alone. When she isn't working or enjoying her downtime, Stephanie tries to give back to her community.

SO HERE WE ARE IN THIS MOMENT, READING THESE WORDS. Let them sink in for a moment: When it comes to time, this moment is all we have. It took me a while to completely realize this fact and incorporate it into my belief system. For many years, I suffered from addictions and mental illness. The last four to five years of my illness were the worst. I was isolated, trying to make it through each day, and still working my full time job, all while thoughts of the past or anxieties about the future ran rampant in my mind every minute, every second. For the last fifteen years, I have been living in recovery. Through a lot of work and life experiences, I came to realize that I was simultaneously trying to control the future and change my past — two things that I now know are impossible. In that time, I have learned to let go and live in the moment because the present moment is all I have.

When I was young, I had a mindset of "live hard, die young." So I always thought I would most likely pass when I was around thirty years of age. This is not the ideal way to look at life, but lots of folks with addictions view life this way in their younger years. This viewpoint allowed me to not worry about getting older or preparing for my future. If time would cease to exist for me at thirty, why take care of myself, mentally, physically, financially, or spiritually? This attitude carried on until I was twenty-eight years old. When I achieved sobriety, I woke up and realized my viewpoint was off . . . way off.

Throughout the years I wasn't in treatment for my illness, I missed out on a lot of opportunities and did nothing to improve myself. When I started living in recovery, I looked back on all those missed opportunities and believed I could make up for lost time. It took me a couple of years to realize the sheer absurdity of this plan: There is no way to make up for lost (past) time. Time is constantly changing, and it is impossible to get back. I had to change my mindset regarding how "far behind" I was compared to others my age. I am always in the right spot at the right moment because I am there. The person I have become because of the illness I experienced is a tenacious, non-judgmental, and compassionate person. There is nothing wrong with that.

This experience has allowed me to work toward my dreams one minute at a time. I ensure my goals and values align while I take daily action toward them. I am invested in the journey, not the outcome. This means I enjoy everything I do while working toward my goals. I cannot guarantee anything in life except my attitude while living minute to minute.

Minute By Minute

I learned the saying, "Take it one day at a time" while I was in recovery. Some days I needed one minute at a time because being sober was scary and I felt overwhelmed most of the time. I was introduced to meditation, which paved the way for me to get centred and not feel so anxious. At first, I found it quite hard because I could never shut off my thoughts. Once I realized meditation was about recognizing my thoughts and bringing my attention back to my breathing, it became much easier. My meditation journey showed me how my thought process and mindset are intertwined. I soon learned to become aware of my negative thoughts and to challenge them with facts from my daily living. Don't believe everything you think. I had proof that I was not as horrible as my mind (addictions) wanted me to believe. Eckhart Tolle uses the term "the watcher;" I began observing my thoughts and realized I did not have to react to them or even respond to them. Over time, I learned that I could reframe and redirect these thoughts, which enabled me to live in the present moment and be at ease with my emotions. I was no longer wrapped up in my overzealous imagination about what the future may hold. I was truly in the moment. I still practice meditation and find it vital to keeping my mind calm and serene. If I had never been sick, I doubt I would have followed this path to freedom from my thoughts, which provided me with an opportunity to grow and reframe my thought processes and bring a conscious awareness to the present moment.

Lost Time

In early recovery, I was determined to make up for my lost time. I wanted to go back to school, work full-time in my career (social work), and volunteer in my community. I also wanted to read every book I never did in my youth, you know, the classics. With this workload, I was barely sleeping and my health was suffering as a result. I wasn't making the time to rest or refuel my body, and I was burning out fast, but I felt I had so much to make up for! I believed I could make up for fifteen years of missed life. It took me a couple of years of wearing that Superwoman "S" on my chest to realize I was slowly killing myself. I was burning the candle at both ends by multitasking and taking on too many commitments, without getting much finished. I began to realize that I had extreme expectations of myself and that what I was expecting to accomplish in two short years was an impossible feat. Comparing myself to others was a waste of time and energy on my part. I had to use myself as my own measuring stick — compare where I was ten years ago, or even one year ago, to the present day and see how much I had changed and grown for the better.

Change In Attitude

My "live hard, die young" belief system did teach me to enjoy the moment as often as I could, but I was doing it in a destructive way. I suffered for all my decisions in favor of instant gratification without any concern for my future self. Thank God I got clean and sober and changed my attitude toward life and time. I stopped planning my own funeral and started to have hope for my future. In fact, having a long future became my desire. My altered perception of time and how much of it I had left in life made me aware of many things. I needed to treat myself like a sacred garden and tend to myself with the same love and care I extended to everyone else. I needed to nurture myself and take care of all areas of my life, and do it in a kind and loving way. I learned that I am worth taking care of and have so much to offer to this world. If I want to be of service and help others, I need to put my health and well-being first. If I do not take care of myself, no one else will, and I won't be able to help others or do what I want in my lifetime.

A large part of me felt like I did not deserve to be healthy and vibrant since I hadn't looked after myself for so long. But that neglect stemmed from my illness, not from a lucid standpoint. Everyone deserves to be healthy inside and out, to strive to be the best version of themselves.

Since entering recovery, my whole perception on life has changed. My new attitude is to live long and serve others. With this mantra in hand, I work on improving myself every day by doing the best I can every moment, in all that I do. Eating well, exercising, travelling often, surrounding myself with positive people, and learning new things regularly are all part of my self-care. This way of life keeps me inspired, intrigued, happy, and serene — a far place from where I once was. I am better for doing these things and in turn, so are those with whom I surround myself. I believe that what I do in this world has a ripple effect. What I do can change the lives of others all over the world. I believe in raising the collective consciousness through positive thinking and acts of kindness. If I were to smile at someone and wish them well, this can change their attitude for the day and influence how they interact with others, and so on. Who knows how far that chain will go and how long it will last! If I can inject positivity in someone's life, then I have used my time well.

Hopes And Dreams

To ensure I am on a path that will help me reach my hopes and dreams, I have created a five-part system to make sure my goals and values match. I believe if what I'm working toward does not reflect my core values, then I am wasting my time.

We never want to feel like we have wasted time, so try this process to ensure you are using your time wisely.

IDEAS: A Five-Part Process

I = Intention. What do you want to accomplish in life? What are your hopes and dreams?

D = Details. Look at all areas of your life: personal, professional, emotional, physical, and spiritual. Where do you see yourself in one, five, or ten years?

E = Ethics. What do you value? Family, community, health, etc. Do your goals match your values?

A = Ask. Will this benefit my family? Will this move my career/business forward? Will this enhance my community? Will this spark personal growth? Will this make me money?

S = Steps. What do you need to do to get there, step by step? Map out each goal and what needs to happen to make it a reality.

When I can see my IDEAS on paper, it helps me figure out *how* I can make my hopes and dreams a reality by putting the pieces together and coming up with concrete daily goals. I know I am not "wasting time" because I am using my time in a way that expresses my core values.

Remember that life happens, and give yourself the flexibility to tune into how you feel every moment. Know that there is nothing wrong with changing your hopes and dreams. They evolve as we evolve. It is a good idea to check our IDEAS on a quarterly basis to be sure we are still on the right track. Nothing is written in stone; it is all fluid. We change and grow, so why can't our dreams evolve alongside us?

There's a saying: *"Youth is wasted on the young."* We are constantly changing and growing from our experiences. I know I have grown from both my years of illness and my recovery. I learn when I am ready for the lesson. Fast-tracking is no longer an option for me; I will never get those fifteen years back, but the experience made me into the person I am now. And frankly, I like who I am. I cannot say I would be here if I did not go through those dark days.

I no longer look back with regret; instead I live in a constant state of gratitude. I feel so grateful for all life has to offer me, moment by moment. I see things in a way most people can't, which allows me to help others in a unique way. I see my experiences as a gift rather than a curse most days because I can support others who are in the same situation. I believe we are all here to support one another, and this is my way of being able to do that. I can help in many other ways, but what a special gift to be able to share recovery.

If you are feeling like you have wasted time, ask yourself, *Am I using my time wisely now? Are my hopes and dreams aligned with my values? Is my time precious and not wasted now?* You have this moment: here, now, the present. How will you use it? I hope you keep dreaming and growing and while doing so, continue to help others on their journey.

~ *I have come to a place in my life where I am now comfortable being fully open about myself and my life. I am grateful to my close friends who show support beyond measure, my co-authors in this series who inspire me daily, and the Creator for making everything possible in life. I am blessed beyond words and hope that my chapter might inspire or give hope to another. Thank you to those who are reading this; without avid readers like yourself, I would not have my dreams come true.*

Timeless Practice:

◇—   Gratitude Exercise   —◇

A great way to enjoy life is to live from a place of gratitude. You can make this happen by maintaining a daily gratitude list. Every morning, write out five things that you are grateful for. These do not need to be large or profound things; they can be the smaller things in life. Some examples are a good cup of tea, the sound of rain on a skylight, the stars at night, flowers, health, friendships, etc.

Use this template to keep on track every morning. If you start your day in gratitude, then you will most likely stay in this state most of the time. Come back to this list and use it to center your thoughts and bring your awareness back to your present moment.

◈

◈

◈

◈

◈

◈

◈

◈

CHAPTER 14

_____

Voices Through Time

_____

BY FALON JOY MALEC

"Don't give up on your dreams. You've
come so far, accomplished so much.
Remember who you are."

~ Falon Joy Malec

Falon Joy Malec

———————

www.lifesdirtysecrets.com

www.essenceofgaia.ca

ig : @lifes.dirty.little.secrets. | @essence.of.gaia

fb : @fjmdesignsinc | @essenceofgaia2018

· · · · · · · · · · · ·

BORN IN ONTARIO, CANADA, FALON GREW UP SURROUNDED by the lakes and wilderness of the well-loved Muskoka region. Here she developed her love of the wild, raw beauty of our Mother Earth and all the creatures that live within her. Falon feels deeply connected to the planet and considers herself to be an Earth Witch, instinctively attuned with both fauna and flora alike. It is this love and connectedness that has inspired her to pursue a path in wellness with a focus on herbalism.

Falon is also a lover of the visual arts. She enjoys painting in her downtime and finds it to be extremely therapeutic and soulfully nourishing. As part of her desire to help others heal, she has also begun a new journey into a Therapeutic Art Life Coach Certification. Her goal is to help those who are struggling with emotional blocks to overcome their demons and find their way back to a well-balanced and positive life. With a deep love and respect for those in positions of service to our country, she plans to one day offer special services to the souls struggling with post-traumatic stress disorder (PTSD).

Falon has been a lover of books since she was a young child, so it is no surprise that she would eventually open herself to the possibilities of writing. Raw and authentic, she shares her passion for life and explores her spirituality, sexuality, and emotional discoveries through her blog, *Life's Dirty Secrets*.

Falon is spiritually guided, believes everything happens for a reason, and is learning to trust the process and enjoy her journey . . . as long as there is coffee.

_____

Building The Layers Of Life

When we are under pressure, we let all the negative words, failures, and mistakes from our past run rampant in our minds, allowing them to tell us we are *not good enough, not strong enough, not worthy enough.* They come forward in moments of fear as *"what-if's"* and *"should-haves."* We shrink in on ourselves and beat ourselves up over every little mistake, instead of focusing on the good in our life and the growth we have achieved.

All of our life moments build up layer upon layer of joys, trauma, achievements, and heartache, whether we realize it or not. Your wins and successes, like the meaty, fleshy bits of an onion, build you up and make you who you are, in all your beauty and strength. Each time, you grow bigger and more intentional in purpose. But those not-so-wonderful moments become those slippery, filmy layers between the good stuff that allow those wonderful hunks of substance to slip away when the knife applies pressure. Each time a layer falls away, the onion shrinks.

These painful moments in time may not even be of our own doing. They could manifest themselves in the form of bullies who, in their own brokenness, cause us pain and break us down into smaller, weaker versions of ourselves. *Never forget, it is not you who is broken.* **It is them.**

Around the age of fourteen, I regularly contemplated suicide. My family was in pieces after my parents divorced. My brother and sister lived with my dad, his wife, and her two sons in the house I grew up in and loved dearly. That was "home" for me, filled with all my childhood memories of birthday parties, staying up late with the Ouija board, and playing house. Memories of Christmas time with us as a family, silver tinsel hung across every doorway, the fresh scent of pine filling our noses and mingling with the smell of fresh baked cookies and brewed coffee. Lights dancing through decorated limbs on our Christmas tree and windows. It was Easter mornings with my siblings, rushing to find all the eggs before they did, trying to get the fullest basket even though mom always emptied them into one bowl anyway. It was my brother shadowing my dad, wearing his little leather tool pouch and helping fix windows and cupboards. It was my baby sister with her tight little curls and angelic little face cuddled between my brother and me watching movies, my friends fawning over her sweet nature. It was sleepovers and Halloween, rushing to eat dinner, get into costumes, carve pumpkins, and go trick-or-treating.

I, on the other hand, lived outside of town with my mom and her husband, in a house where I never felt I belonged. Everything was white and crisp with few photos on the walls because no memories were shared there. Even my room felt like it belonged to someone else and my things were just in it. My stuffed animals piled atop my storage trunk in the corner of some other girl's room, while pictures of my childhood hung on her walls.

I wasn't speaking much with my dad at this time and as a result, I didn't get to meet my new sister for the entire first year of her life. I missed everything during her little baby stages, and it gutted me that I didn't know who she was. I disliked my dad's wife from early on in their relationship and resented that I had to accept her in our lives. Trying to avoid her, I would go out with friends whenever she visited, but she would get offended and complain to my dad about hurt feelings, and I was told to stay home whenever she visited us. Fine. I would stay in my room.

It was lonely living this way, so I thought being with my mom would be better. She was always so active in our lives, taking us to Brownies and Girl Guides and becoming a Brownie leader. She helped us with crafts and earning badges. Took my brother to his beaver and cub meetings. Sewing and knitting, she made clothes, doll clothes, blankets, and quilts. Her new husband, however, was a terrible human being who enjoyed causing us emotional pain every way he could.

As a lover of art, I channeled my feelings of loneliness and depression into drawing and sketching. A pencil sketch of an old beat-up tire swing hanging from a gnarly old tree on the edge of a grassy cliff during sunset, hidden on a shelf in my room. It was how I felt at that moment — alone, beaten by the storms of life, and on the edge of living and dying. The title written in the top left corner: "Lost and Alone."

While I was out, my mom's husband decided to go through my things and found my sketch. He wrote on it, destroying one of the few elements that kept me sane, leaving me a message to find the next time I needed some therapy. "It's your own fault you are alone."

It was summer holidays, and my mom and her husband were out. Hopping on my plum-colored six-speed, I peddled myself to the highway overpass a few kilometers up the dirt road by our house. The sun was warm on my skin, the breeze cool on my face as I flew up over the bumpy road. Fresh grass recently mowed by a neighbor and the faint odor of freshly spread manure from the nearby farmer's field filled my nose. I laid my bike against the weathered concrete barrier and looked down to the highway below. The stone rough and warm beneath my palms as I leaned over, watching as cars of all shapes, sizes, and colors, transport trucks with their thunderous horns and roaring motorcycles, revved beneath me, completely unaware of my existence. I was there to jump. Standing there, staring at the white dotted lines below me, broken against the dark, worn out concrete, I thought, *It is my fault. He's right. I should jump and be done with it. No one would care, they're not here with me. They wouldn't miss me. How long it would take them to notice I wasn't home…?*

A Guardian Angel

My Grammie was my angel. My saving grace. From the time I was two years old, she would pick me up each Sunday, dressed in her finest blouses, pressed pants, and baubles of costume jewelry. Smelling of *Imari*; strong and floral, she would surround you in a blanket of spice and wildflowers. Each Sunday she'd ask, "Are you Grammie's little Angel or are you Grammie's little Imp?" To which I'd reply, "I Gammie's Angel."

While I am not overly religious, being more spiritual than anything in my thirties, it was the teachings of Grammie's church that gave me pause. I was afraid that the pastor was correct — I would suffer more in the afterlife, be even more alone, if I took my life for granted. Her love for my soul saved me from jumping that day.

After a series of unfortunate events, more words from "family" telling me I was "*no good,*" "*incorrigible,*" and "*a problem,*" there was a period in time when I was drifting in the wind from place to place: a friend's house, then another, then another. Grammie always came to my rescue. Even though at the time I didn't think I needed it, nor did I want it, now I am grateful. She was a life raft saving me from what would have been a very different future, drowning in misery, drugs, and Goddess knows what else.

Grammie was also the reason I finally got to know my baby sister. Frustrated with the way our family was behaving, she would have none of it. Whether we liked it or not, I was joining her when she visited for the holidays and my sister's birthday. *That's what family does, darn it!*

My baby sister took her first steps down the same hallway I ran down as a kid, dressed in her blue velvet dress with white lace trim, her soft brown hair in a bow and curled in one large ringlet. Her beautiful, brown eyes sparkling mischievously over a toothy grin as she realized she was now unstoppable. My heart was full watching it!

I wanted to be there. I wanted to know her and be with my siblings where we belonged, in the home where I grew up, our memories alive within those walls. So with Grammie's help, I asked to move back home.

Layers Slip Away

After a few months, we were moving into the new home my dad was building. It would be larger and accommodate all of us better than the little bungalow I loved. We got to help build it! Once the ground was broken, we helped construct the footings for the basement. We helped with framing and painting. Hands are even stamped into the floors in the garage, forever marking our existence — just like our childhood home. I was excited and hopeful for our future together. It wasn't where I grew up, but it would be ours.

Things didn't go as I envisioned. I still didn't like my dad's wife, but I did my best to get along with her so I could be with my family. It was incredibly difficult for a long list of reasons. My diary, like every eighteen year old's diary, was riddled with reasons why I despised her and how I loathed pretending otherwise. It held the truth of my thoughts and my feelings, none of which I dared to speak out loud, except occasionally in edited versions with Grammie.

This intimate and sacred space that I kept for myself, safely camouflaged amongst stacks of other books and journals, managed to find its way into my stepmother's hands, and she proceeded to read every sordid detail. Afterward, she sat the family down for dinner, putting me at the head of the table — not in my usual seat, but in hers. She announced her feelings toward me now that she knew my real feelings for her. She told us she couldn't live in this house with me in it, knowing how I felt. Either I went or she went. She promised I would spend my life alone, as I was a terrible person and no one would love me this way. Perhaps because I was still a kid, or perhaps because I was lacking self-confidence and was seriously unsure of my worth in the world, this has stuck with me my entire life, casting shade on everything I've lived through since.

It didn't matter that I was a good student with teachers praising my writing or artistic abilities. It didn't matter that I appeared in a local newspaper with a photo of one of my art pieces or that my art was put on display in a local gallery. It didn't matter that I had friends or a sweet country boy who called me every night to talk about our day — who made me feel special. All I heard was *their* voices echoing in my ear, *"You're not good enough. No one will love you."*

Out of fear that they were right, I jumped at the first chance at what I thought was love.

We met at work when I was preparing to go on an adventure out West. After a year together, I believed we were in love and he decided to join me on my journey across the country. Together, we braved the February blizzards and minus-forty degree weather, arriving in Edmonton three days later.

My knight-in-shining-armor then transformed into a manipulating narcissist, spending the next five years running around with women he met online while I tried to build a life for us.

I did everything I thought I was supposed to do to keep his love directed toward me. Every meal cooked from scratch with fresh, homemade bread baked each weekend. The house was cleaned so much that my fingers and knees ached from scrubbing everything by hand. I made his lunches, supported his business endeavors, and put my own hobbies on hold to save for his, in case they failed or needed more funding. I loved his son like he was my own — and still do, missing him to my very core to this day. They were my family. My heart. I just wasn't his.

He would tell me I was stupid and call me an idiot when I did something incorrectly. Raging and yelling, he'd throw and smash our belongings around me when I didn't follow his orders or refused his requests.

I wanted to leave. I wanted better than this. *Other people didn't live this way, so why should I?*

And then I would hear the voices of my past, calling from three provinces away: *"You're not good enough. You're going to be alone."* When I tried to ignore them, I would hear his voice, *"You're stupid. You won't make it without me. No one else will want you."* And so I stayed.

Sometimes An Ending Is A Beginning

When I was headed home from work one evening in April 2008, my dad called while I was still in my little Sunfire. I was pulling up to the last set of lights, with our apartment building around the corner. The light was red, so I answered and put the phone on speaker. Something was wrong; he rarely called during the week. He waited until I had pulled into my parking lot and turned off the engine to tell me my Grammie had a heart attack the night before and was in the intensive care unit (ICU) in Toronto. She was alive, but hooked up to machines to help her breathe.

As I listened in silence, hot tears pouring down my face, he told me details of what had happened. It felt as if all the breath had been knocked out of my lungs. I was shaking so fiercely, I could barely disconnect our call and remove my keys from the ignition. "Please God," I begged, "don't take her from me!"

Eventually, Grammie woke up and started breathing on her own, but I was panicked trying to figure out how to get home. All of our finances were wrapped up in my fiancé's endeavors. Everyone told me to wait, everything would be fine and to not concern myself with flying home just yet. Stupidly, I listened.

One weekend in May 2008, I woke to a call from dad, and my heart stopped. Rolling over in bed, I stared at the call display for a few seconds. My dad's number kept flashing. *If I don't answer, it's not real.* Terrified of what I already knew, I took a deep breath and answered.

My beloved Grammie had passed away during the night. She'd signed a DNR request earlier after a wonderfully animated visit with my Auntie. She knew it was time and was ready to go home to her Heavenly Father and join his angels. Even if we weren't.

Her death shook the very earth I stood on, and something in me broke. Hearing the words "she's gone" ripped my heart into pieces; the physical pain of losing her was unlike anything I had ever felt before. I rolled over in bed, curled into myself, and screamed into the pillows with all the rage and agony that came with losing the only person who had ever stood by me. I couldn't breathe, it hurt so much. My heart was literally broken.

Standing over her at the visitation, she laid peacefully on satin, as if asleep. Her soft, wrinkled hands were folded delicately across her chest, hands that had held me, giving me strength when I was afraid. Hands that had wiped tears and runny noses. Hands that had taught me to bake, cook, and preserve. Hands that had plucked crisp, fresh peas from a garden and plunked the plump, green pearls on my tongue as a child.

Her hair was white and her skin pale. She didn't look like herself. She'd stopped coloring her hair some time ago and had lost so much weight. She had literally begun to wither away during the time I was gone. I had just left her behind, taking for granted that she would still be there when I returned. Now it was her turn to leave me behind.

It's your fault you're alone. You should have never left her. You didn't even come to say goodbye. See how terrible you are. Those words, those voices played their tune in my head, over and over again, like a broken record that would never stop.

Months after the funeral, still broken in my grief, I was convinced everyone was lying. She wasn't dead. Couldn't be. There was no way that was her in that coffin. Haunted by dreams of her, locked away where I couldn't save her. Always just ahead of me in the distance, I could never reach her before she disappeared around a corner.

I needed her strength to help me through this, and she wasn't there.

At least . . . not physically.

I Believe In You

I never knew Grammie's husband, the man who fathered my dad and his sisters. From what I've learned over the years, I wasn't missing much. A lousy father, a worse husband, and a drunkard hardly around, he treated the register in Malec Shoes as his own personal bank account.

When my dad was just a wee boy, Grammie found the strength to leave her husband, all three children in tow, during a time when women just didn't do that.

With the support of her siblings, she moved out, saved some money, and bought her little modular in a park just outside town. The modular where I spent the first two years of my life and many summers with my cousin. The modular where she had her heart attack.

Grammie is the strongest, kindest, and most loving person I've ever known. She was at every birthday, every Christmas, every Easter. She never missed a school play or graduation. She never let you feel unwanted or unloved, and she did her darndest to keep you safe and make you feel secure. Her strength and light was so powerful, she would carry you when you couldn't, believing in you when you didn't.

Looking back now, I realize that when I finally decided to leave my fiancé, it was her strength that got me through it. If a woman with three kids could do it in the 1970s, I could do it as a single woman in 2010. It was her voice I heard, whispering *"You can do it. I believe in you."*

However, living on my own for the first time in almost six years, feeling as though my dad's wife was right, I was struggling emotionally. Suicide looked like a better solution for me yet again. Sitting on my couch, wrapped in a pink and white crocheted blanket my mom made, crying from the loneliness and fear of failure — it was Grammie's hands on mine pulling me out of the darkness, reminding me, *"You are not alone. You are loved and always have been. I am here."*

Even now, as I begin my journey as an author and entrepreneur, struggling with the fears instilled in me from my past — fear of failing, being alone, and not being good enough — it's her unwavering love that reminds me: *"Don't give up on your dreams. You've come so far, accomplished so much. Remember who you are."*

Who Am I?

I am the fourteen-year-old kid who decided life, as painful as it can be, was still worth living.

I am the nineteen-year-old girl who sought adventure, packed her bag, drove across the country to a city she had never been, with no job, no home, and only a few hundred dollars in her pocket.

I am the twenty-six-year-old woman who realized she deserved better and found the strength to stand on her own two feet, even if it meant being alone.

I am the thirty-year-old woman who was stubborn and determined enough to ignore the naysayers, work her ass off, and buy a house, on her own.

I am the thirty-three-year old woman who became an author, decided to begin her own business, and put into motion the plans that would allow her to eventually quit her nine-to-five job and do all the things she wants to do.

No longer am I made up of layers of good and bad, allowing the negative to build barriers between my successes and eat away at me. Instead, I am a freaking diamond, compressed over the ages into an unbreakable substance that will survive and stand the test of time. And so are you!

Grammie was a lighthouse in a storm. She was a rock to stand on and the glue that held our family together. She was a living, breathing angel. Like all angels do, she gave me her wings so I could fly.

"I love you," she whispers, "Grammie's little Angel."

~ To Shawn, Shannon, and Magin, thank you for being my reason to keep breathing. You've been my reason to live more times than you know. Thank you to my mom and dad for giving me that breath. Grammie . . . my guardian angel, thank you for showing me how to use it.

CHAPTER 15

The Face Of
The Beast

BY JULIE CHESSELL

"Setbacks will never define
my comebacks."

~ Julie Chessell

Julie Chessell

ig: warrior.bossbabe | fb: julie.l.chessell

JULIE CHESSELL IS AN INTERNATIONAL MOTIVATIONAL SPEAKER, published author, and passionate entrepreneur. She is an associate with the Proctor Gallagher Institute, a successful blogger, and defines the meaning of a Warrior Momma. With her extensive knowledge of the healthcare field as a registered nurse, she vows to assist people during their darkest and most joyful moments. Her greatest and yet most challenging role to date is being a mom to three incredibly talented boys and a soulmate to her husband, Chris.

TIME — A SMALL YET CRUCIAL WORD IN THE HUMAN VOCABULARY. A way to track the days, weeks, months, hours, minutes, seconds, and milliseconds that mark our existence. Time — a word that polarizes us. We think we have either all the time in the world or none of it at all. Just like a hamster running on a non-stop wheel, we try to get off the "busy" bus and endeavor to slow life down or, in some cases, speed things up. We go about our daily routine, almost mindlessly, until one day we become painfully aware that there really is little that we can truly control. We realize that time has a constant ebb and flow; it waits for no one.

If we listen closely, we may hear the Universe's whisper to us, but we usually ignore it. We are sometimes so unaware of our surroundings that we need the Universe to slap us in the face and say, *Hello, are you listening, I'm trying to get your attention!*

I try very hard not to relive or replay the last 480 days over in my head, but I still do. When I quiet my mind and heart, I realize that sixteen months' worth of emotion need to be acknowledged, embraced, and felt. I go back to the hamster wheel analogy. I was trying to be the perfect wife, the perfect momma, the perfect sister, the perfect friend, the perfect nurse, the perfect hockey manager, the perfect hockey executive, the perfect business woman, the perfect leader . . . the list goes on! In the end, trying to be this perfect person cost me more than I ever would have imagined.

For months, I had ignored a major life-changing moment for more important things . . . work, hockey, a trip to St. Lucia with my hubby, lack of sleep. All of these things were more important than what was right in front of me . . . Can you relate?

I share my story with you, and what a powerful one it is, not for sympathy or pity but rather to empower and heal one another. This is a story of how **setbacks will never define my comebacks!**

I wrestled with the decision to travel to Las Vegas last year, April 2017. I knew it would be a lifeline for my business, but I had no clue how I would afford to pay for it. Not to mention, the kids were busy, and I would miss my oldest son Carter's thirteenth birthday (that tugged at my heartstrings). But I didn't want to disappoint my business partners, and that voice within me just kept getting louder and louder: *Go, you need to go!* And so I went . . .

The red-eye flights did me in; can we say tired and raccoon-eyed? I felt incredibly guilty about missing Carter's birthday, missing hockey, and spending the money on this trip. Yet in hindsight, that weekend was my saving grace. Thank God, I got sick on the plane. Thank God, I vomited all the way from the airport and also called in sick to work that night, something I never do. Ever.

Why thank God, the Universe, or Source? I give thanks because after months of constantly ignoring all the signs and messages, I was forced to become focused and present and take a look at a problem that the Universe had been calling me to pay attention to. Finally, when my focus was all in, all there, I received the harshest reality check, a chain reaction of events that changed my life and the trajectory of my family's life forever.

I never dreamed that when I called in sick to work that night, it would be the last time I returned to work in 2017. And as I share this with you, I only recently returned to the workforce, almost a whole year later.

I've always said that out of my three boys, Brock, my middle son, would be my jailbird . . . or in other words, the one who causes me the most grief. He has always been the one to test the waters, find amusement in pushing our buttons, and delight in knowing he was right (even when he is wrong, which isn't quite often). In April 2017, he was diagnosed with a life-altering illness: cancer. It was a sucker punch straight to my gut, shattering my heart into a million little pieces. Could I have seen this coming? Probably not.

From time to time as moms, as a family, as a society, we look back and wonder what we missed, and *how* we missed it. We reflect on how we could have been so blind as to not notice anything, especially the little things. For example, if we didn't get the job we wanted, we think, *What if I didn't answer their questions more intelligently?* Or if we can't fit into the perfect dress for date night, we think, *What if I worked out harder? Why did I eat that? What if it makes me gain all this weight?* "What if" becomes the catch-all phrase we relish in and then use to blame ourselves for the outcome.

As a mother, my role is to protect my family so their hearts won't be broken. I am supposed to take away their pain when I can, as much as I can. But this time, this one time, I just couldn't do that. I couldn't be the one to fix their problems. It took me down a self-reflective rabbit hole: *Nothing in life ever flows smoothly, at least not for me. Nothing is simple and nothing goes according to plan. I have been tested often in my forty years, but this was by far my biggest test to date.*

Yet I couldn't ace this test. I didn't know the answers to everyone's questions, including mine. I was supposed to be the glue, the voice of reason, the pillar of strength and calm. I was his mom. I am his mom. I should know how to fix this, yet I can't. Nobody could, except time.

For five whole days post-diagnosis, I sat there trying to fix this. I wanted this to just disappear, be gone. Poof! As a mom, you always guilt yourself, doubt yourself, question yourself: *What did I miss? Why didn't I act sooner? This is all my fault! How can this happen? How can I remedy this? How could I not be the protector that I'm supposed to be? What did I ever do in my life to deserve this much pain? Why was this happening to my family, to my child?* You lie awake at night and regurgitate all the events that led up to this moment. This life-changing, forever earth-shattering moment.

As a mom, I also needed to be strong, not display any emotion, because my little bubba fed off my energy. If I displayed strength and calm, he would display bravery! I wanted answers, and I wanted to simplify it for my family, for Brock. I went into a "Let's get 'er done" mode. War paint on, strength as my armor, love as my healing balm, and a positive focus as my bullets of choice to attack this miserable disease.

I just wanted more time. Time to breathe, time to interpret what was happening, time to be with this beautiful soul who was facing the greatest and most challenging fight of his twelve little years on this planet.

I realized that I was no longer in control. I was at the mercy of a ravenous disease that did not care about age or life span. This was a disease that thrived on the negativity and distress it brought. It reared its ugly head and made its presence so well known that life as we knew it ultimately collapsed. That was the intent of this beast, and I was staring down its tunnel. A long, dark hole of uncertainty. I had the true, unwavering notion that it was in charge, it would determine fate. But even though this supreme being was in control, it didn't have to dominate our daily existence. That would only happen if we let it.

I was going to make time work for us. How? By finding focus and balance. As a child, my mother had instilled in me a sense of being fair, kind, resilient She was a single mom on a path she had never dreamed of, but she was resilient and supportive and prided herself on forging on to make both of her children's lives fair and equal. Whether it was Christmas presents or her time, she always found a balance between her two children.

During those first two lonely and scary days in the hospital, while our world was falling apart, we had to remember that we still had two boys at home. Thirteen-year-old Carter, who had access to technology on an hourly basis, and eight-year-old Rhettster, who only knew that his momma and Brock weren't home. How on earth does one duplicate normalcy when it no longer exists?

Upon hearing the diagnosis that Wednesday, my mind immediately shifted to *How are we going to facilitate a conversation with the boys about what was happening?* Without involving Brock too often, we decided when his siblings came to visit him for the first time, we would take the plunge into reassuring those little brains about a diagnosis that we ourselves had not yet come close to processing.

We mandated a theme within our little family and preached it over and over that afternoon: *Cancer eats negativity and hates positivity.* We broached the subject very calmly and very matter-of-factly: this was just a bump in the road. We included Brock in this dialogue because ultimately, he needed to hear these words . . . over and over again.

I remember a very poignant moment when I told Brock that he would never be defined by the diagnosis. I instilled in all three boys the belief that this malignant illness fed off of negativity, grew off of defeat, and relished in adversity. This was not going to be our story! In turn, we made a family pact that this beast would now be upstaged by us. We were not conceding to the notion that this was our destiny. We needed to fight with every fiber in our being; the alternative was not an option.

My heart was breaking, and I didn't believe in what I was preaching. All I knew was that infinite time was not on our side. As a momma bear who feels her sole existence is to serve and protect her babies, I knew we needed to make the most of the present space that we had together. And so our story began!

We decided to not constantly live in fear because we did not know how much precious time we had left. Decide has a sound, like an ah-ha moment or ringing in the ears. That ring was so loud that we could no longer ignore it. We consciously made that choice to live each moment to the fullest. Each day brought new growth and an unknown journey. We didn't know where the end would bring us, but we knew what the middle would look like. It would be a middle filled with laughter, positivity, a warrior mindset, and an overall attitude of "We've got this!"

Don't get me wrong, I was realistic in my dreams. You see, the funny thing about time, at least when you have been given an expiration date so to speak, is that your planner extraordinaire comes out in full force, even if it is for something that brings you heartache. Instead of planning for his milestones such as birthdays, first dates, prom, graduation, college, wedding, and many more, here I was, silently planning things in the background without giving away an ounce of my sadness and grief to anyone around me. I knew where Brock was going to be buried. I envisioned the songs the choir would sing and the type of celebration of life that he so deserved. Never once did I speak of those plans. These plans were for my mind only. I did not intend on ruining the unmistakable joy we were desperately trying to find.

We travelled, we swam, we shopped, we snuggled, we ate ice cream for break-fast, we had parties, we shaved our heads, we told one another we love each other every chance we got. We stayed present in every fleeting moment. This is how we passed the treasured time we had.

Fast forward sixteen months, and here I am, sharing our journey of resiliency, ferocity, determination, and love. Many parts in our lives have been enhanced by our journey this past year. We have learned numerous lessons, and are still com-ing to terms with many others. No one has a crystal ball — if only we could foresee our future before it finds us.

I am often asked if I would change anything. Trust me, I have pondered that an-swer on many levels, on multifaceted planes of existence. The honest and truthful answer is no. No, I would not modify anything. No family should have to go on this scary, dark voyage, but I am so grateful for the path we chose to walk because of the lessons we encountered together. Maybe that sounds crazy, but things al-ways happen for a reason. Would I have believed that statement in the early days of last spring? Hell no! Do I resonate with it now? Yes! One of the greatest lessons in all of our pain and triumph is that no one person can be prepared. Life is like a carousel. It keeps spinning round and round and stops when you least expect it.

We all live and breathe by the perpetual notion of "We don't have enough." Not enough money, not enough friends, not enough clothes or shoes (or maybe not the latest trends), and certainly, not enough time. Only when we are faced with mortality or uncertainty do we become truly cognizant of the time we have always had at our disposal. The need to hurry up and get somewhere doesn't matter. What matters is *how* you spend your time. Your mindset sets the tone for your life — having a warrior mindset and taking charge of your life gives you back the time you think you didn't have.

Be aware of your life, my friends! Learn to recognize what it is showing you before you get hit so hard you cannot recover. Use your God-given talents wisely. Love true and hard. Support and encourage those who love you with the same fierceness and kindness they show you.

We can never truly appreciate the time we have until it is taken away from us, or at least the possibility of it. Your mindset is everything. Being that positive light will come back to you tenfold. Live each day as if it were your last. Brighten someone else's day, take chances, and do not fall into the trap of "someday" or "live for tomorrow." We all know that tomorrow is not guaranteed and that someday is too short to build a lifetime of memories. Memories, love, life are all built on the founda-tion of your present moment and on truly savoring those moments with your loved ones. Live your life to leave a mark in this world. Carve your legacy, your imprint, and make sure that it's one to remember. Slow down and breathe, and don't miss the cues that are right in front of you because you are too busy to notice them or care. Time is precious. Never take it for granted. I'm so humbled and grateful that I paid attention and learned how to finally cherish every single moment.

~ I want to send my deepest gratitude to my husband, Chris, who has encouraged and supported this journey from conception. Thank you for never letting me give up! To my three boys, Carter, Brock, and Rhett, you teach me on a daily basis what unconditional love is and you allow me to strive to be a better human being. I'm so proud to be your momma. I also could not have done it without my family and friends — this journey isn't possible without you all. To my Golden Brick Road Publishing sistas and family, your patience and expertise has made me grow and shine in ways that I never thought were possible. Finally to the beast we all call cancer, thank you for waking me up from slumber and forever changing the pathway of the life we now lead. I am grateful and humbled.

Chapter 16

A Premature Lesson In The Value Of Time

"I am sure you have heard the quote,
'Take it one day at a time.' For me,
sometimes even one day was too big a
time frame. Some days, I have to take it
one hour at a time. And that is okay."

~ Charleyne Oulton

Charleyne Oulton

---

www.coachcharleybrown.com

ig: coach.charley.brown | fb:charleyne.oulton

· · · · · · · · · · · ·

Portraiture by: Katie Jean Photography, Mill Bay, BC

CHARLEYNE OULTON IS A CONFIDENT AND HAPPY MOM of three children who lives on beautiful Vancouver Island, BC. She is genuine, experienced, and passionate, as well as an appreciated health and wellness coach, published author, blogger, and photographer even through the busy and beautiful chaos of raising a family. Charleyne birthed premature children who would spend months in the Neonatal Intensive Care Unit. It is her purpose to inspire women, and specifically the busy, overworked, and exhausted mothers around the world, to count their blessings and realize that each and every second of their life and the lives of their children is a miracle and not something to be taken for granted.

THERE ARE 86,400 SECONDS, 1,440 MINUTES, AND 24 HOURS IN ONE DAY. Your entire life can change in one single second. We need to realize and remember time is measured not only by clocks but also by moments. As a mother of three children who were born very premature, I have learned to value how powerful a **minute**, an **hour**, or a **day** can be.

I was only seventeen years old when I conceived my firstborn son. I experienced unexpected preterm labor and was given shots of steroids and antibiotics to help my unborn child's lungs develop. Every **hour** he remained inside my womb was an hour that gave his lungs the chance to produce more surfactant, thus reducing his risk of lung issues. My son Jaiden was born at thirty-two weeks gestation on November 18, 2004 and spent twenty-one days in the various levels of the Neonatal Intensive Care Unit (NICU). He was flown in the ambulatory helicopter from our local hospital to a larger general hospital where they had the ability to help preemies with issues like his. From the very first hour of his life, he was not a "healthy" or "typical" baby. Sadly, Jaiden spent a lot of his early years in and out of the hospital being seen by doctors. He was prone to bronchitis, suffered with childhood asthma and Respiratory syncytial virus (RSV), and seemed to catch every single cold out there. The hospital often felt like our "home away from home," but he was a wonderful and calm patient, and this was our normal. Finally when he was around eight years old, we discovered that all his health issues were directly related to a rare disease called Mastocytosis. Jaiden struggles with atypical asthma, allergies, and idiopathic anaphylaxis and even had a mastocytoma tumor removed from his back. He is a warrior and a fighter through and through, and this was evident even when he was only an hour old.

When I was in preterm labor with my next pregnancy, I learned the value of a single **minute**. I had been flown from our general hospital to a women's hospital on mainland Vancouver in an ambulatory Learjet because there were no available incubators or rooms in the NICU at our local hospital for a preemie as early as our son was. My water had ruptured and my labor was inconsistent, but progressing. My contractions were not showing up consistently on the monitor, and we could not do many more internal examinations because this could cause stress or infection for my tiny unborn child. I was completely alone. My partner at the time had to stay home with our son, who was a toddler and could not fly with me. It was just me and my unborn child in the labor and delivery room, in a hospital that was not ours, living through a birth plan that was not the one I had "planned." I could sense that the nurses were starting to feel very frustrated with me. They had other patients to tend to and here I was: exhausted, extremely emotional, telling them that I was about to deliver my baby and something was wrong, but the tests were not showing anything. I am not lying when I say I must have pressed that little red alarm button attached by a cord to my bed about twenty times an hour. Thankfully, my nurses did come to me every time, and the last time I called them over was the beginning of my delivery. The baby was breech; he was entering the birth canal and his heartbeat was erratic because of his size and the stress of labor. I was terrified and in extreme pain, and even at this time, the contractions were inconsistent on the monitors (which is very normal for premature labor). The nurse ran and got the doctor, who did the fastest internal exam I've ever had and told me in a very steady but concerned voice that we were headed for an emergency c-section. This all took about three, chaotic minutes. I felt such relief though, because finally somebody believed that I was, in fact, in active labor. I actually signed the procedure forms while being wheeled to the operating room. I was put out for his delivery. There was no time, and he was in distress. I was told he was delivered in less than six minutes. My son Jeffrie was born at twenty-eight weeks gestation on January 23, 2007, and he spent thirty-five days in the various levels of the NICU. He was my healthiest baby. He was put on room oxygen and was breathing strongly, for a little preemie. The hardest part of his NICU experience for me was when I was discharged and able to go home but had to leave him all alone in a city and hospital that was only accessible to me by plane or ferry. I had a toddler at home and needed to heal from surgery. Jeffrie spent almost two weeks in the hospital he was born in, until he was stable enough to fly home to our island's general hospital. Jeffrie has had a few health issues from being born so early, but nothing significant. He simply needed more time to grow and develop. He was alert, active, breathing well, and had a feisty spirit, and deep down I knew he would be okay from the very minute I first laid eyes on him.

"Do not boast about tomorrow, for you do not know what a day may bring."
~ Proverbs 27

With my third child, I learned the value of a **day**. With this pregnancy, I was put on bed rest prior to the delivery. I had two very young children with compromised immune systems at home, and being pregnant and trying to care for them proved to be a big challenge for me. If any of you reading this have raised a toddler and a baby at the same time, you will understand the gorgeous chaos of a house during this chapter of life. It was no surprise that this was a juggling act because I was not able to care for anyone, under doctor's orders.

My water ruptured at around twenty-two weeks, and I spent the next month admitted to the hospital being monitored closely on complete bed rest. This was one of the hardest experiences of my life to date. I battled insomnia, guilt, depression, and anxiety. I felt completely helpless, and yet each day that my daughter stayed inside my body was a triumphant victory. Every single day she grew stronger, healthier, bigger. Her body, organs, and brain developed a little bit more. I leaned very heavily on my support network at this time. I needed their help to raise my babies back home, to help out with the housework, to come visit me, to lift my spirits up. My daughter, Juley-Anne, was born on February 28, 2008 at twenty-six weeks gestation, and she spent fifty-six days in the various levels of the NICU. She was born with a chest deformity called Pectus Excavatum, as well as a heart murmur, but was born quite healthy. Because she was my third baby in three years and three months to go through the various levels of the NICU at our general hospital, I found the process familiar and almost comforting. With any preemie, you ride a rollercoaster of emotions, from fear, anxiety, and pain to joy, celebration, and love. I cherished every day I got to be with her in the NICU, for it meant she was one day closer to coming home.

My children were all born sick and with health issues. Their "tomorrows" were not promised or guaranteed. I've seen my children suffer and live in pain, be intubated, breathe on CPAP machines, need oxygen, and go through surgery, illness, and many recovery periods. They have all been hospitalized numerous times and sadly, we were well known at our local hospital when they were little. What I have come to realize through these experiences is the importance of living in the now. I am sure you have heard the saying, *"Take it one day at a time."* For me, sometimes even *one day* was too big a time frame. Some days I have to take it *one hour* at a time. And that is okay.

There are moments each and every single day that deserve to be appreciated and celebrated. You must learn to find these little moments. For these are the ones that truly matter.

It's the little moments in life that make raising children truly magical and enjoyable. Going outside together, beachcombing, camping, hiking, gardening, lying in bed cuddling, puddle jumping, watching a movie together, reading a book, sharing a meal, receiving random hugs, I love you's, and messy written love notes . . . These are a few of my favorites. Experiencing these moments are a reminder

Timeless Practice:

◇— Here is an average week for most people: —◇

Sleep 8 hours x 7 days = 56 hours

Work 8 hours x 5 days = 40 hours

Life (eating, showering, driving, kids, friends, gym)

5 hours x 7 days = 35 hours

Hours not accounted for = 37 hours per week / 5 hours per day to follow your dreams, learn, make positive change in your life.

◇——— What does your week look like? ———◇

Sleep __ hours x 7 days = ___ hours

Work __ hours x 5 days = ___ hours

Life __ hours x 7 days = ___ hours

= ___ hours per week left over to follow your dreams, learn, make positive change in your life

Now divide this time by 7 to see how many hours per day you have available, take it one day at a time!

◇— Tips: —◇

- utilize your social media time by joining a positive group online or enrol in a program
- turn family and friend time into productive learning or hobby time, instead of tv. Involve them in what you are doing or want to do.
- prep some meals in advance, to spend less time in the kitchen a few days per week
- see if you can carpool
- use your lunch breaks productively to read, do yoga, or listen to a podcast about what you are interested in

SECTION 5

CHANGE THE COURSE OF TIME

"Good comes to those who wait . . . but
good is created by the ones
without patience."

~ Ky-Lee Hanson

FEATURING

Maryann Perri

Janelle Mason

Ky-Lee Hanson

CHAPTER 17

The Sign

BY MARYANN PERRI

"We are creatures of habit. Though
that is ok for the most part, I find it
sometimes prevents us from varying our
experiences and prohibits us from
adding value to our lives."

~ Maryann Perri

Maryann Perri

Connect with Maryann on any of these social media outlets:

ig: maryannperri

fb: facebook.com/maryannperri

. . . .

MARYANN PERRI IS A SELF-PROCLAIMED "SUPER-MOM" WITH a big heart and empathetic approach toward people. She is an overachiever with an abundance of energy and an overzealous love for life and adventure. A graduate of York University with a post-graduate diploma from Seneca College, she majored in corporate communications, landing several exciting jobs along the way. She married her high school sweetheart in 2002 and soon after moved to Mexico, where she dedicated herself to teaching English. Fourteen years, three kids, two dogs, and an entire new circle of friends later, Maryann mastered speaking Spanish and developed a love for the Mexican culture, food, people, and country. Her husband and her children, Cristian, Mia, and Alexia, are her pride and joy. Full of spunk, laughter, and passion, Maryann deems life to be an adventure that one must continuously challenge. She always fills the room with her big personality and believes we are not meant to live life in a "square box;" rather, we must take chances to add zest and variety to our journey. She feels change is necessary for our development as human beings. Her goal is to drive people to find their happiness. "Everything happens for a reason" is her mantra, and she has found that tragedy has allowed her to see the good in every situation. In her free time, Maryann loves to cook, travel, exercise, read, and spend quality time with her friends, family, husband, and children.

I'VE HEARD IT TIME AND TIME AGAIN: *"Be careful what you wish for."* I never quite understood what this meant, until it happened. I still remember that moment like it was yesterday. I had just driven home from work through traffic and a crazy storm and was walking through knee-deep snow to get to my front door. As I shivered and struggled with my bags and keys, all I thought was, "Please God, get me out of here, take me somewhere warm and less chaotic."

Just a few months later, my husband Vince was presented with an incredible opportunity to move to Mexico for work, and before I knew it, the sign was up and our move was becoming a reality. No more contemplating, no more deliberating! We made the decision to up and leave for a couple of years; there was no turning back. Our house would be sold, personal belongings packed, and all our possessions would be placed in cardboard boxes waiting for us to claim them again.

A few weeks before we were scheduled to leave, reality suddenly sank in, and I broke down and cried. I was afraid of the unknown! I was afraid of leaving my friends and family! *Learning a new culture? A new language? What was I thinking? Was I ready for this?* My friends knew their mission the following day would be to come over and cheer me up. We ordered Chinese food, sat outside, and talked about it all. After they left, I lay in bed thinking, *What would I do with my time in Mexico?* I panicked.

The following morning, I turned on my computer at work and much to my surprise, a random message by poet and essayist Joseph Addison popped up on my screen. The note read: *"Three grand essentials to happiness in this life are something to do, something to love, and something to hope for."* My heart beat fast as I read the message. I thought, *That's true, thanks for letting me know, sir!* In my new venture to this foreign land, I knew I had two of the three main ingredients, but lacked one! Something to love? I had plenty of that. Something to hope for? Also covered. But what about the key ingredient: something to do? How would I pass my time? I was so used to having structure and a methodically organized schedule, I felt helpless thinking of the unknown. Without "something to do," would I be missing a main essential piece to happiness in my life? I knew I had to figure out which direction "the sign" was pointing me toward. I decided to find a job as an English teacher.

"The bad news is time flies. The good news is you're the pilot."
~ Michael Altshuler

My life in Toronto was not going to be "my life" anymore. By the end of the month, we'd be leaving it all behind. I started to feel a surge of emotions as the final day fast approached. I was scared. I reminded myself constantly that new experiences lead us to be the people we are today. Life isn't about settling, dwelling, and waiting; it's about making things happen while trying to maintain a positive outlook, no matter what comes our way. Let the past be gone, use it to move forward, use it to make the future better. It's like a *limited-edition game* at which we only get one shot, so we need to make each moment count. That was my goal as our new adventure finally began . . .

Our experience in Mexico was *increíble!*
I found it amazing how people truly enjoyed their lives and how relaxed everyone seemed. I got a job teaching grade four in a private bilingual school close to our home. Ready as ever, I remember having my first "teacher meeting" the week I started. I made sure to get to school with plenty of time to spare to ensure my prompt arrival. To my surprise, the rest of the teachers calmly strolled in fifteen minutes late, laughing and conversing. So casual, so carefree — you'd think it were their cultural mantra. After fourteen years of living in Mexico, it became slightly contagious. I try to have the same carefree, nonchalant attitude — "try" being the operative word. Mexicans take special pride in the fact that their culture emphasizes a very laid-back and casual approach to life. Maybe this method isn't necessarily adaptable in Canada, the U.S.A, or other parts of the world, for many different reasons, but perhaps we can take it with a grain of salt and try to incorporate some of their values into ours.
"Viva, baila, y besa la vida" (Live, dance, and give life a kiss). Wouldn't it be nice to live in constant *fiesta* mode!
We all agree money can't buy happiness — or at least that's what many Latin Americans say. The *2018 World Happiness Report* has shown once again that some Latin American countries have a higher happiness index than developed nations in Western Europe. What is it about these regions that make its citizens happy? The answer seems to point to invaluable assets, such as friendship, family, and religion, which constantly enrich our lives, making them fuller. These are things that money could never replace. According to *The 2017 World Happiness*

Report, countries that experienced significant economic growth, such as the United States and China, suffered declining levels of happiness. Latin America, on the other hand, was an exception — its happiness level was above the global average and the highest among developing regions.[7]

We can all agree that income is a component of happiness; we can't deny that, yet happiness is sometimes greatest in the poorest countries where people can't meet their basic needs. After a certain income threshold, more money does not guarantee more happiness, which may help explain why happiness in Western countries varies little over time.

If money isn't everything, what else makes Latin Americans happy? An IDB book on quality of life in Latin America and the Caribbean spoke about the cultural aspects that help explain the region's levels of happiness. To begin with, the region's cultures value happiness and personal satisfaction more than many other cultures. For most Latin Americans, time spent with friends and family, along with strong religious values, can be more important than standard of living, education, health, work, or housing.[8] Interestingly enough, the concept of happiness has been debated for over 2,500 years, but idea of "happiness" linked to economy only began 400 years ago. Latin Americans, specifically Mexicans, clearly respond to the concept of "happiness" with a perspective that predates to the economic one.[9] Family, friendship, and religion are key to their happiness; hence they worry less about being so structured with their "time" in order to make more of it for social interactions.

Now that we're back in Toronto, I feel I have a different perspective on things. Life as I knew it for fourteen years has changed drastically. I can't say I'm entirely thrilled to be back, nor can I say I'm entirely unhappy. It's just distinct, as our two worlds collide. I miss my friends and life in Mexico. I miss it a lot. But I continuously tell my kids that life is an adventure; it's about living through change, going through hardships, and conquering new challenges. At times we are happy and at times we are not — life is about learning and adapting. We must not look at battling challenges as an obstacle but rather as an opportunity to discover and grow as individuals, taking on bits and pieces along the way.

I struggle with the illusion that time is nonexistent. I myself am guilty of constantly complaining, "I have no time!" And then I stop and tell myself, "No, stop, you do have time!" I'm just not making enough of it for the things that truly matter, and I have a misconstrued ideology of what I need to focus on most.

7   World Happiness Report. (2017, March 20). *World Happiness Report 2017*. Retrieved from http://worldhappiness.report/ed/2017

8   IADB. (n.d.). Retrieved from http://www.iadb.org/en/research-and-data/publication-details,3169.html?pub_id=B-632

9   Why Are Latin Americans Happier than Their GDP Would Suggest? - Ideas matter. (2017, April 20). Retrieved from https://blogs.iadb.org/ideasmatter/2017/04/19/latin-americans-happier-gdp-suggest

Recently, my cousin's father suddenly passed away. After getting home from being with the family that evening, I thought to myself, *Isn't it odd? The only time we get to see our entire family as a whole, including extended aunts, uncles, and cousins, is when someone dies.* Seriously? Why does it have to be that way? If we have "time" to drop things in an instant and gather around to console and be together during difficult times, why can't we do that more often, under happier circumstances?

I never realized how busy life in Toronto would be. The lifestyle here is definitely fast-paced, more than what we were used to after living in Mexico for so many years. Maybe it's the distances people have to drive, maybe it's the amount of extracurricular activities we think we "need" to have our kids participate in. Maybe it's just the need to feel like we are doing something more than the person next door. We are overplanning, overscheduling to the point where our smartphones have become our best friends and personal assistants, limiting our precious "time" for things that really matter! We have programmed ourselves to believe our time at home must be used productively, and by that I mean *(in my personal experience)* doing household chores, driving my kids from dance practices to soccer games, auditions, grocery shopping, bath times, bed times, and so on.

We are constantly rushing, and in doing so, we are only focusing on getting things done and not living in the moment. We must let go of the "rush" and step back to allow ourselves to experience feelings like joy, connection, and love. I know it may seem impossible to do at times, but if we are able to consciously slow things down every now and then, we are bound to find our inner stillness and a sense of peace. Aren't we?

We are creatures of habit. Though that is ok for the most part, I find it sometimes prevents us from varying our experiences and prohibits us from adding value to our lives.

Most of us can agree we often feel our days are vastly different yet shockingly the same. The framework is very much alike every single day, but the conversations and moods are so very different. I'm sure we can also agree, scheduling the day according to a **routine** is a surefire method to ensuring each day is consistent. Though it is most commonly effective for babies and children, I think as adults, we too can appreciate a repetitive schedule. Think about your comfort level with activities and events when you are familiar with them and know what to expect. One can argue, *"Routine is boring, repetitive, dull or tiresome."* Maybe sometimes, but I think it's what keeps us going . . . *and to those with children — it's what keeps us* **sane!** I would pick boring and sane over exciting and insane any day, wouldn't you? Or maybe not!

While it's great to have a routine, something to keep things in order, there isn't a specific template set in stone. What may work for one person may not exactly work for the next. We need to allow ourselves to be more mindful of the bigger picture. By doing so, we can consciously start making life adjustments to achieve our goals for the future. Do we ever stop and think about where we are in life? Are we happy? Are we serving our purpose? Are we making the right decisions? Are we following our heart's desire? What really matters? The answer is simpler than we think.

News flash! It's okay to break out of your perfectly established routine — occasionally! This is where my experience in Mexico comes into play. The difference between how time is used there and how it is used here is that in Mexico, it doesn't matter what day of the week or time of day it is — friends and family always make the time for one another. A once-a-week coffee gathering is inevitable, and surprisingly enough, even events such as birthday parties or bridal showers are often organized mid-week. Even though people in both countries have the same "running around" to do, folks there are far more flexible and not so stuck in a square-box-routine like we sometimes are here.

"Vive, ama, y se feliz" (live, love, and be happy)! Isn't that what we all want?

It's up to us to make it happen.

Take a trip, plan a night out, go for a long walk, have a picnic, sign up for that dance class you always wanted, enjoy life as best as you can. It's important to stop and smell the flowers occasionally — or often! So go ahead and plan a birthday party or a play date on a Tuesday night. Change up the routine on Wednesday. Make plans with friends at the last minute, without overthinking. Maybe it's time we stop and consider if our "goals" are the right aspirations that deserve our time and energy. Don't be afraid of change; it's good! It helps us become agile, flexible, and adaptable and reveals our strengths, which is something we will learn to appreciate more and more as we grow older and wiser.

A while ago, I had gone to a doctor's appointment and when leaving the office, I came across an elderly couple walking hand-in-hand slowly to their car. As I smiled and held the door for them, the gentleman looked at me and said, "You'll be like us one day, dear." While most people dread getting old, my initial reaction was, "I hope so, sir, what a blessing it would be." Because it would. And although growing old would be lovely, it's not necessarily the length of our time on earth but rather the quality of how we live our lives that will count in the end. If for a moment we can close our eyes and picture ourselves frail and gray, what is the one accomplishment we would be proud of? Would we stop and think about the jobs we had (or didn't have), or the cars we drove (or didn't drive), or the fortunes we made (or didn't make)? Or would we stop and remember the life experiences we shared and the memories we made with our loved ones? To succeed along the path of our life, we need to live in the moment and make each experience meaningful and count for something significant. Let's not be afraid to change things up a bit; it's what will keep our minds active and guide us to discover who we are, both inside and out. Let's value our loved ones and consciously grasp the idea that life is too short. Even though at times it seems endless, it does go by quickly.

From the moment we are born to the moment we take our last breath, we are given "time" to make our lives meaningful and worth something. Naturally, we try to set goals and visualize achievements as we make our way, day to day, month by month, year by year through a structured lifestyle. All this is great, but we must not forget that success is also about being able to break out of old habits every now and then. We need to use our own judgments, stop feeling societal pressures about how things "should be done" or "need to be done," and just *let them be!* I've always been a true believer in the saying, *"Everything happens for a reason."* Maybe it's too cliché, but we must make a conscious effort to follow our instincts when we feel overwhelmed and overcome with a sense of desperation. If you feel like you have "no time," take a deep soulful breath and look at it as though the Universe is telling you something important, sending you a *sign.* Maybe slow things down a bit, make a change. Although time feels endless, it's ticking away, and our *mindfulness* is what will help keep us successfully moving forward! It's *time . . .*

~ Gracias Mexico! You taught us how to cherish family, value friendship, and always challenge a difficult situation with a smile and sense of humor. You accepted my family with open arms and never made us feel "foreign." Gracias a nuestros amigos y compadres por siempre estar a nuestro lado y por enseñarnos tanto sobre la vida. To my amazing husband, Vince, and awesome kids, Cristian, Mia, and Alexia, you guys are champions in all you do, big or small, and continue to teach me about life and myself on a daily basis. Thank you for being an incredible source of positive energy. I adore you and feel blessed to be on this journey together. Thank you for your support and for being my inspiration. My family, my clan, my heart.

Chapter 18

Six-Minute Increments

by Janelle Mason

"From even the deepest of heartaches and greatest of tragedies, we are gifted with a lesson and given the chance to experience growth."

~ Janelle Mason

Janelle Mason

www.janellemason.com

ig: janelle_mason_ | fb: JanelleMason.Success.Coach

. . . .

JANELLE MASON IS A BUSINESS COACH AND MOTIVATIONAL SPEAKER. From the age of nine, she dreamed of becoming a lawyer and after fast-tracking her degree, she graduated at the age of twenty-one with a Bachelor of Law from James Cook University and a Graduate Diploma in legal practice from the prestigious Queensland University of Technology in Australia. She spent most of her twenties practicing law in Australia and around the world, and in 2014, she obtained her Master of Laws while living in London, the place she now calls home.

When Janelle was twenty-eight years old, she suffered a heart attack and nearly died. Struggling to reinvent herself and figure out her purpose after that wake-up call, she spent years in a quarter-life crisis of unemployment and depression. Eventually, Janelle discovered her true purpose as a coach for female entrepreneurs and now runs a successful coaching company in London. She's on a mission to empower one million women to identify their true purpose, live happier lives, and make an impact in the world with their business. As a young woman living with heart disease, she works closely with charities and hospitals to raise much-needed funds and awareness, especially for heart disease in young people. Her dream is to empower women globally to live happier, healthier, and wealthier lives through her coaching programs and speaking engagements. You can find her talking business in her free Facebook group for female entrepreneurs, "Ambitious Business Women," and chatting health and lifestyle in her free Facebook group, "Heal Janelle's Heart."

I REMEMBER LYING ON AN OPERATING TABLE IN A TOKYO HOSPITAL, wide awake, as two doctors in green scrubs worked tirelessly to save my life. I was twenty-eight years old, and I'd had a heart attack.

Just twelve days before, I had been at home in Australia after finishing a two-year contract traveling the world as an in-house lawyer, when I started feeling sick. At first, I thought it was just a cold. I was in the shower and noticed it was hard to breathe. I literally had to open the shower screen, hang my head out the door, and take a deep breath of fresh air before going back in to finish the job.

I vividly remember how confused I felt in that moment, having to gasp for air like someone would do before diving into a pool. To not be able to breathe in the shower was weird, but once I was out, I could breathe normally and the problem sort of went away, so I didn't overanalyze it too much.

The next sign I got that something wasn't right was when I was trying to make my bed. I had been a diligent bed-maker for as long as I can remember (a habit I thank my parents for), but now I had to stop half way through the three-minute task just to sit and catch my breath. I mean, what twenty-eight year old needs rest breaks while making the bed?

Again, I pushed the concern out of my mind and told my mum I thought I had a cold. I remember saying, "It's like a cold with no cough." I wasn't feeling 100 percent, but I also didn't feel like I was dying or that it was urgent enough to need to see a doctor, so I pushed on.

As the days wore on, the signs that something wasn't right got more frequent, but let's be clear, there was no clutching-the-chest, numb-left-arm, fall-on-the-floor-in-a-dramatic-*Grey's-Anatomy* moment. It was just shortness of breath and some pain between my shoulder blades. I thought it was a mild flu, as I hadn't lived in a country with a winter in over three years. It seemed to make sense in my mind, so I put it down to something that would pass and continued about my day.

The next time things got pretty bad was when I was walking across the Story Bridge in Brisbane. Not entirely a short walk, but it's no Mount Everest either. I was about halfway across the one-kilometer walk carrying my overnight bag over my right arm when the pain in between my shoulder blades got so bad that I actually stopped walking, turned around to the direction I came from, and analyzed whether I'd better off turning back and calling a cab.

In that moment, I was more worried about what other people would think of me, a fit-looking young woman stopping in the middle of a busy pedestrian bridge and struggling to walk, rather than feeling concerned about what could possibly be wrong with me. Once again, the concern was squashed when I got to my friend's house and sat down. I'd made it, and as long as I wasn't moving, the pain went away, so I didn't think much of it. I had a glass of wine with my friend (as one does before jet-setting overseas), and that was that. When my mum dropped me off at the airport for another one of my overseas business adventures, she actually asked if I was going to be okay. In typical Janelle style, I reassured her that I felt fine and that if it got worse I promised to see a doctor in Japan. So I flew ten hours on a plane to Tokyo and spent another seven days putting up with the pain and shortness of breath as I struggled to walk even short distances.

Thinking it was muscle pain, I grabbed some of those stick-on heat packs you can get over the counter at any pharmacy. I put them on my shoulder blades but they didn't do a thing (kinda obvious, really)! So I got a massage. As the masseuse was putting some elbow grease into my deep tissue massage, I felt the pain go away. After ten or so days of what was now pretty annoying back pain, I'd finally gotten some reprieve. Or so I thought.

When the massage was over and I got off the table, the pain came back right away. In hindsight, that massage could have dislodged the clot and killed me instantly, right on that massage table. I've never been that religious, but the only explanation I can come up with for surviving that massage (and indeed, for surviving the entire experience) is that something far bigger than myself somehow was at work and watching over me.

Finally, I took myself to see a doctor. With my friend translating, the nurse explained that the doctor (an older gentleman who didn't speak a lick of English) wasn't sure what was wrong so he gave me an antibiotic and told me to come back tomorrow to get the test results. Because I found sleep next to impossible, I was also told it was safe to take a sleeping pill so I could get some rest that night.

After taking the prescribed antibiotic and two sleeping pills, I still wasn't able to fall asleep. By this point, my mum in Australia had been informed that things were getting worse. In a broken, slow, and painful voice, I sent her an audio message telling her that I was going to go to the emergency room.

Listening back to those messages sends chills down my spine. It was clear I was in pain, but if anyone had seen me, it wouldn't have appeared that I was dying or close to it. My friend even tried to talk me out of going to the hospital because, well, you know how those places are, you wait for hours and hours to be seen and in the end you're given nothing but paracetamol and instructions to rest (insert eye roll).

I almost reconsidered my decision to go to the hospital, but my intuition was telling me I had to go. I can't explain the feeling, but the nudge from within was strong and my inner G.P.S. was clearly saying, "Janelle, get to hospital now." So I listened to my instincts and called a cab.

To their credit, the hospital staff saw me pretty quickly and put a rush on the test results. As I sat on the floor waiting for news, I realized I'd reached my limit. The pain between my shoulder blades was so unbearable at that point that I was pounding my fist on the chair telling my friend, "This was it." I'd reached my pain threshold and I needed to see the doctor right away. I was pleading with the Universe, with God, with my friend, with anyone who would listen: "Please, please, please get the doctor, I can't handle this anymore."

It had been about twelve days since the first signs of heart disease had reared their ugly head, from the first moment I had trouble breathing in the shower and making my bed, to sitting there on the hospital waiting room floor, begging for some kind of miracle.

Just then, the double doors swung flying open and about six nurses and doctors came rushing out. Before I could blink, I was in a room on a stretcher struggling to understand what was going on as a nurse held a disposable razor in my face, tugging at my track pants.

Someone managed to translate that I'd had a heart attack, that I needed a stent in my artery, and that they had to shave me "downstairs" to prepare for the procedure. Despite the circumstances, I managed to make a joke as I told them that "downstairs" was all taken care of (thank you very much!) and that their shaving services were not needed.

It was all happening so fast, and I realize now there was a huge sense of urgency to get me to the operating room, but I had to call my mum and let her know what was going on. She freaked out, naturally, and through my tears, I said, "They want to stent me like Dad . . . I have to go now, I'll call you back." I handed the phone to my friend with instructions to keep my mum in the loop as the nurses pushed paperwork in my face, pointing to where I had to sign.

Now this is where the lawyer in me kicked in. Despite the gravity of the situation (which I didn't fully comprehend because most of the talking was in Japanese), I wanted time to read the document and make amendments before signing. My friends who were translating said there was absolutely no time for that. They urged me to trust the doctors and just sign the document. Reluctantly, but with immense gratitude now, I did.

I decided this was a good time to mention I didn't have travelers' insurance (I know, I know, Murphy's Law — the only time I've travelled without it, and look what happened). I promised the doctors that I'd get myself checked as soon as I got home to Australia and asked them to let me go because I was not insured. They looked at me quizzically, as though I had lost my mind, and said (through translation), "Janelle, we don't care that you don't have insurance, if we don't operate right now, you will die." I blinked in complete shock. By this point, my friend was crying, but my tears had dissipated. I was in deep shock.

Maybe it was a blessing in disguise. Perhaps my lack of understanding gave me a sense of courage, which in hindsight, I desperately needed to get through the next couple of hours. Before I could call my mum back, they took me into surgery. I lay on that operating table stark naked, feeling isolated and bare. With nothing but a local anesthetic in my wrist, I felt a warm tingly sensation as the doctors gently moved the balloon instrument from my wrist up my arm toward my heart.

I remember pleading with the doctors to tell me what was going on, begging them to help me breathe. I was telling them, "I can't breathe, I can't breathe" as I wiggled on the table in unbearable pain, but nobody answered me. I now understand it's because they were focused on saving my life (I guess they're forgiven!).

To say I'd left things to the eleventh hour was an understatement. The procedure, which ideally should have lasted an hour, lasted for a full two. The clot was so hard from being there for such a long time that it took twice as long to break through. Watching my heart on the monitors in the operating room, I saw the moment they broke through the clot. What had been a white patch of oxygen-starved heart muscle suddenly filled with black, streaky lines. The blood was pumping back through my heart and at that moment, the doctors said to me, "You should be able to breathe now."

What had presented as flu-like symptoms some two weeks before was actually a 100-percent blocked artery. Because I'd neglected it for so long before getting medical attention, I had killed 40 percent of my heart muscle. Although it's repaired itself now, the post-surgery scar tissue and signs of damage to my heart will always be there. No amount of time will heal those wounds because the damage was so severe.

My whole life, I had worked hard to climb a ladder I thought I wanted, only to find it leaning against the wrong wall. I fast-tracked my degree, qualified at age twenty-one, practiced law, and traveled the world. I knew from the age of nine that I wanted to be a lawyer, and I was the first in my family to go to university. I was the kid who was always organized, excelled at everything I did with perfection, loved pleasing people, and preferred reading books to watching TV or going to the movies.

My favourite gift when I was fourteen was an alarm clock gifted to me by my parents for Christmas. It was pretty simple for what it was back then, but I loved it and thought it was the bee's knees. When that alarm went off in the morning, I would leap out of bed and be the first one in the shower. I loved living my life by the clock and as a lawyer, working fifteen-hour days was something I wore as a badge of honor. I thrived on the pressure of tight deadlines and an overloaded schedule, getting kicks out of managing a workload that others thought impossible.

As a lawyer, you're recording every minute of your day with precision and diligence, focused on "chargeable time" and six-minute billable units. "Making budget" and "meeting your billable hours" was lingo that seeped into every lawyer's vocabulary, especially at the end of each month. Living by the clock was a habit that most newbies had trouble adapting to, but for me, it was something that came oddly naturally. I loved it (I think secretly I've always loved "time").

Recovering in intensive care with plenty of time to think about my life and the massive wake-up call from my near-death experience gave me a new outlook on time. Suddenly I was mortal, and six-minute increments had a new meaning.

The thing I've come to realize about working too much is that you tend to replace the things that matter with the things that don't. You no longer have time for the gym. You stop seeing your friends and start eating dinner at your desk. You tell yourself that you *don't have time* to pee, let alone to see a doctor if there's an ache or pain. You put things off that should be prioritized and miss out on having fun and living each day like it's your last, because you think you've got tomorrow. But what if you don't?

"Realize deeply that the present moment is all you have." ~ Eckhart Tolle

Have you ever said, "I'm too busy" or "I don't have time for that" or "I'll do that when I retire?" Let's face it, we've all said something along those lines but the truth of the matter is, it's not about time. What you're really saying is that *thing* isn't important to you right now. In that very moment, you're making a decision and choosing something else, and *that* decision is delaying your dreams, your success, and ultimately, your happiness. At the end of the day, spending time stressing out about the future (which you can't control, by the way) only leads to panic and overwhelm. The only moment in time that we can control is the present moment. *This* very moment.

You see, after my massive wake-up call, it took me a while to view it as a wake-up call, as something I could learn a lesson from, a turning point in my life. For a long time, I was depressed, I desperately wanted an explanation, and I felt sorry for myself. Although I got a job in retail and moved cities with that role, I wasn't living up to my full potential. I was trying to sort out my life, but in truth, I was lost and playing small, stuck inside my comfort zone. Despite graduating from the "Ticker Club" (a four-week rehabilitation course with sixty- and seventy-something-year-old men), I was scared that doing anything even remotely risky would lead to another heart attack or worse, to my death.

I eventually managed to find an inner strength that reminded me of the girl I used to know pre-heart attack. The courageous, fly-by-the-seat-of-her-pants girl. So I leaped into the next adventure and moved to London for a job opportunity. It was in that moment I knew things would shift, because I was stepping far outside my comfort zone, away from familiar territory, away from family, friends, and my doctor. I still wasn't entirely happy and often used alcohol to drown the sorrows of a bad day, to hide my emotions, and to stop feeling sad about how shitty my life was. Despite living in my own apartment with a pretty cool job in one of the most amazing cities in the world, I kept focusing on all the negativity, on what I didn't have, which left me feeling unfulfilled.

It took three years following that wake-up call for me to realize it was indeed a blessing in disguise and to finally find my purpose in life. I stopped practicing law, reduced the stress in my life, hired a life coach, and launched a business. What I have learned from this journey is this: everything that happens to you actually happens *for* you. I've discovered that from tragedy and heartache, your true genius can shine, and the journey to that discovery can be your biggest gift if you learn to embrace it as a lesson instead of judging it as something bad.

Time, a concept invented by overzealous lawyers with expensive watches, is not something to be measured in six-minute increments. It should be measured by the impact you create in the lives of others and in the world, and the happiness and fulfillment you derive from doing so. Working as a coach with female entrepreneurs and spending my days aligned with the joy my work brings has given my life a greater meaning. I'm no longer available to procrastinate on my dreams. I embrace each moment like it's my last, consciously taking action as my heart desires and turning my dreams into reality each and every second of the day. I know for sure that if tomorrow never comes, I'm grateful for the second chance and thankful for all of life's lessons that cross my path.

~ I wouldn't be writing this if it weren't for my four special friends in Tokyo that fateful night. To you, I owe my life. From the deepest part of my heart, thank you. To my husband, for your unwavering support and for believing in me more than I believed in myself at times, thanks, baby. And a very special, heartfelt thanks to those doctors who saved my life and the nurses who put up with me escaping their watchful eye to sunbake in the car park, causing my heart monitor batteries to die, cracking jokes at every chance I got, and basically being a royal pain-in-the-ass of a patient. From the bottom of my not-so-broken-anymore heart, thank you!

CHAPTER 19

All Of The Things

BY KY-LEE HANSON

"Don't worry about your future,
it is in your hands."

~ Ky-Lee Hanson

Ky-Lee Hanson

www.goldenbrickroad.pub | www.gbrsociety.com

ig: kylee.hanson.bosswoman | fb: kylee.hanson

KY-LEE HANSON IS AN "IDEA" PERSON: always seeking deeper understanding and providing new visions to the world. She is inquisitive, self-sufficient, and self-aware. Ky-Lee creates and executes dozen of projects at a time and lends a helpful word and guidance directly to hundreds of people every week. Ky-Lee is very curious about herself, life, and people in general; she finds it all fascinating. Her studies in sociology, human behavior, stress management, nutrition, and health sciences have led her to have a deep understanding of people. She is optimistic but understands things for what they really are. Being someone who can spot potential, one of the hardest things she learns over and over is: You can't help someone who doesn't want to help themselves.

Growing up, she had a difficult time understanding why people couldn't seem to live the lives they dreamed of. Often thinking she must be the main character in a world similar to *The Truman Show*, because nothing seemed to make sense, she always saw things differently and found it challenging to relate to people. This ended up sending her into a downward spiral in her twenties, when she felt she had no choice but to settle. She felt suppressed, limited, and angry. Ky-Lee has the ability to hyperfocus and learn things quickly. She has a power-mind, and found the true strength of life and her endless capabilities through a serious health battle in her late twenties. Ky-Lee took control and, over the years, mastered how to get her power back: mind, body, and soul. She also discovered the best way to "relate" to people is *not to*; instead, simply listen to understand their world for the uniqueness that it is.

Ky-Lee is a multi-time best-selling and award-winning author and a successful serial entrepreneur. She thrives on creating opportunities to help people along their journey, and she excels at it. Her success came by developing the taboo art of collaborative business. Ky-Lee has an open-door policy she learned from her mom, a listening ear, and an opportunity to lock arms and take you down your *Golden Brick Road*. You can absolutely connect with her.

THERE COMES A TIME IN LIFE, ON YOUR JOURNEY OF ENLIGHTENMENT, when you learn to set yourself aside from the ego, the judgement, the doubt. You will also set yourself aside from personal desire and fulfilment. You gain a deeper sense of being and become multi-purposeful. You are many, in one. You can divide your energy and time when you come to terms that you are a mind, you are a body, you are a soul, you are a spirit, you are love, you are an energy. You are many. There is instinct, intuition, and innovation inside of you. At this time, you become more possible; you realize that society is systematic, a bit broken, and resembles a game. You realize your spirit and soul are bigger. They don't fit into this box. You follow your intuition and realize she can take you down many paths at once. You can experience all of the things.

"All Of The Things" has become a fun but also serious saying in my life. "All Of The Things!!!" in absolute excitement and momentum, and "All Of The Things." with a hard period there, when everything is in motion and I am living through them *all*. I believe I have been given this life to experience and learn. To enjoy society, but not to lose my *Self* in the game of it. I have the big house, I have the successful business, and I also have friendships, family, inner peace, and I help many people. I have ALL the things. And I do ALL the projects. I explore and spend time in all the things that light me up, or burn me up. It is understanding the fire inside you and letting it spread.

How did I get here? The truth is, I manifested it. I created a clear picture and asked to see the steps to get there. It is not about wanting and waiting; it is all about the doing. Switching your time toward the "goal" and stepping into it now. I am not a big fan of the word "goal." To me, a goal has an ending and specific requirements to becoming reality. Life is more "growth" than "goal." Sayings such as *Enjoy the journey*, and *It is not about the destination, it is about the journey getting there* have shaped my outlook and helped me to live. Plan instead of wish. Realize you are possible. Become the environment you need so you can grow and flourish; it is all within you. Reinvent and create this new found *you*. BE.

At some point, someone told you to be what you are right now. They told you that you needed identity in this world, you needed a title in this society. Let me tell you that you don't. You are you. Every bit of you makes up a unique being like no other. *That* is you — this is what you can offer the world, the world being collective energy of all people, NOT society's expectations of getting a job, needing more followers, more cars, more money. You can have both, and it comes when you are 100 percent *you*, when you feel into things instead of following expectations. Someone may have told you that you can't, and I am telling you that you can. The choice is yours.

Earlier in this book, Effie explained that we go into states of depression in which we are visiting the past. We are stuck in trauma. We visit states of anxiety which are fabricated, a figment of our imagination, something that has never happened before. We create a fictitious outcome from a state of worry. In both cases, we alter our reality and visit times that are not the here and now. So why not use this power we have, the way we are essentially time traveling with our mind, to positively influence our life instead of only using it for negative manifestation?

Crystal clear vision is exactly this. It is a focused state of manifestation in which you see every detail, you travel back and correct states of mind, you travel forward and put thought into the good outcomes. It is possible to paint a crystal clear vision of destruction and pain, but we need to move away from this thought pattern and shower our thoughts in love and possibility, in self-belief.

My biggest shift occurred when I realized I had a responsibility in this world. My heart has been broken all my life because of the suffering of women and children around the world. It is my responsibility to take care of myself, to fix this heart, and to do so, I have to look outside of myself. I have to help the global energy so I can then feed from its positive charge. When we feel negativity, we need positivity to maintain a balance, and when the global energy is black, we all feel drained. Inward healing is just as much external healing. It is about the environment of energy. If we process negative energy and transmute it into positive energy within us, our brain patterns start writing a different story. Reflection, new perspectives, healing of trauma are all examples of this. We can do it for our future, too. Society has not been all that great when it comes to prevention. We have Band-Aid approaches for most all things: medication, therapy, debt consolidation, the justice system, recycling, etc. We wait until things get bad before we do something about it. We all have the ability to create anxiety; some of us suffer from it greatly and it has control over us. For me, anxiety had to do with hormonal imbalance, diet, substance abuse, my environment, my "goals," and my lack of self-awareness, as well as not understanding my mind as the powerful creator it is. If you are an anxious person, you are seeing into a version of your future. What if we talked down the anxiety and painted the outcome we want to see instead? We can create our worry, so why can't we create our pleasure? What if we can use this discomfort to our advantage? What if the anxiety is a sign that you're in the wrong environment? What we envision for ourselves is often the path we will walk.

Living in a nonlinear way means two things to me: jumping around within our timeline (which we do mentally, affecting our entire timeline) and living many lives at once, doing *all of the things*. An example of the former is holding onto a negative memory of a relationship from the past with a lover or friend. It ended with pain. You can remember that feeling; you can go back and visit those arguments, and you will feel sour the rest of your present day. You might be less trusting suddenly of those around you now. What if you visited that time and changed the conversation, changed the outcome, healed it, had it play out differently, focusing only on the good? You aren't forgetting what happened or creating an illusion, but you are choosing to forgive and remember the good so you can feel better in the now. There is always something you can choose to learn and always something good you can choose to focus on from a bad situation and experience. It could be that you were strong enough to leave or that the opposite party had some ounce of care for you to let you go. It could be how you handled the situation or what you learned from it, how you treat people better now because that experience is a part of your timeline. The memories are yours — you are the only one who sees them, *you* can decide *what* you focus on, *you* can decide *what* message you take from that chapter in your life. You do not have to punish yourself just because you were in a negative circumstance, even if you were responsible for it. Forgiving yourself is the most powerful thing you can do. It is not about anyone else. Their actions were theirs, and we have to proceed in the most self-loving and understanding way. This does not mean we ever have to welcome these people back into our life, but it does mean that we can no longer remain frozen in that feeling. Separate yourself from the situations and focus on who you are now.

In terms of living many lives at once, I am an example of someone who has had many careers, many endeavors, and been many things to many different people all at once. I'm also a great example of not doing things in a traditional step-by-step manner. I tend to start in the middle, get to the end, then go back to the start and build from there. It's hectic, but it's fun and effective. You do not need approval from anyone but yourself. You need self-forgiveness, you need to focus on the positive in your past, and you need to look at the future with clear possibility, not worry. We all are experts at looking at the future with doubt and worry; instead, practice filling your thoughts of the future with hope and determination. When it comes down to it, what are you going to lose by switching the socially accepted negative to a positive? Don't we have everything to gain? The people who truly have unconditional love for you won't go anywhere; you might lose some fake people, but that's a plus! You will gain new love and respect for yourself because you took a chance on *you*, you stopped worrying about every dollar, because what is money, really? It's tangible energy. Are you suffocating your own energy supply?

I worked hard for the material items I have, and I love them. I cherish them, but I am not scared to lose them. It's possible to get everything back. We have to look at ourselves as creators and as thinkers. We can learn, we can manifest, we can build something out of nothing. We are humans, creative beings. This self-understanding has been oppressed. We have been told only crazy people change the world. Come on now, I think it's crazier to have one life and not use it to its full potential. Create within society, create within love and life. Learn about the earth and soul, your connection to it all. Seek new ideas and come to terms with yourself and society. We are always discovering new things; many ways of the day-to-day life we currently lead are not all that old, yet we fully commit to their practices. We do not have it all figured out yet, so the way I see it, we should stop looking for someone else to provide us with the answer. I take all their answers and formulate my own understanding so I can contribute to this seeking and sharing of knowledge. I don't see any greater purpose.

Once you learn to set your personal agenda and self-expectations aside, forget about the constraints of society, and realize you are just as possible as everyone else, you can begin to enjoy and have influence. You can always start over. Reset the clock. Reinvent. You can always learn something new while you do something else. The greatest certainty in life is change. We are born to grow. You can make a new plan, you can heal from the past mentally or physically. It is all possible. Tomorrow can be completely different than today, but if you want to come back to today, to the present, this very moment, it is always here waiting for you. People say time is fleeting, but it isn't. It is there. The future is there; the past is, too. The present is certain, but *you* create the reality of what your "right now" looks like. I am envisioning when this book is out, I am experiencing that feeling months before it actually happens. So who is to say that didn't just happen? I felt it?

I think there is more credit due to the imagination and the dream state. Utilizing these two has made me a master at manifesting. What I think about does show up in my life, over and over. My spouse says it all the time. I express color trends, I pictured a house a lot like the one we have, I manifest wins (and sometimes complications) in my company, and I end up exactly in the visions I intended. I have manifested $30k many times. This can be done through clarity, self-belief, word usage, visualization of the outcomes and desires, and the path to them. It does not have to be logical or standard, or as someone did before you. You **do** need to take action. Just thinking is not enough. You have to put yourself **in** the situation as well. You have to be open to receiving. People think receiving is a good thing, but it is not always an easy thing. We can also receive criticism, closure, pain, lessons, and challenges. Nothing in this world is coincidence. Nothing. If you are after something, opportunities are going to show up that seem odd — those are the right opportunities to take a **new** path. The ones that seem easy, familiar, a surefire bet — those are tests to keep you in the same place. When something seems perfect, forget the "too good to be true" mindset. That is an old way of thinking that got people nowhere very quick! Learn to say "perfect" and "yes" when you feel that click. It's not a bad thing. It's lining you up for what you asked for. You deserve it. The path is being created to teach you how to be ready for it. Take it. Familiarities and distractions are the real "too good to be true" situations.

I am not a person of patience. It's a virtue, I hear, but it's a nemesis to me. It is not that I "want" something now or that I "want" to be or identify as something; it is not about ownership and possession. I just need to start exploring what it is like to get there. I need to live, it excites me. I want to feel the experience. I want to feel the opportunity in front of me. Humans love to look forward to things. Sadly, this love has been burdened by anxiety, as well as society's caution to not try anything unless you are already perfect at it. How do you become perfect? Practice and failure, repeat. Repeat. Repeat. Repeat. Sometimes excitement can be skewed into nervousness and blown into anxiety. When we do this, we are creating something in our mind that has not happened yet, and this act of man-ifestation will influence the actual outcome. Our perception is confused. Anxiety turns into fear, and we then fear being anxious and are stuck in a loop so far away from excitement. Something has altered our time and broken our ability to dream, to create, to use nonlinear living for growth. Patience is the practice of not getting angry while waiting for something. I "get" that it is wrong to get hangry (anger + hunger), but that is human nature. I get that it is wrong to get angry when some-one is late, but maybe it is a sign that they do not value you or that something is happening in their life to make them spiral and they need some help. Our emo-tions are signs of our experience; our emotions are signs that we need to pay at-tention to what is going on here. Controlling our emotions is understanding them and using them as they were intended, as energetic signals. I am not a person of patience and have come to be proud of that. I *do* get angry waiting for something because what I am waiting for, what I want, is social change, peace, a conscious society of creators. I want to see innovation, I need to see human rights, I need to see happy people. So yes, I will get angry and have no patience with this big picture as I aggressively search for every stepping stone of the process.

I am a very literal person; I am a serious person when it comes to the words I speak about my existence, actions, and being. When someone presents an idea to me, I do not understand things hypothetically — to me, it is a waste of time. This is not to say I am not a dreamer, but I am more so a planner and a creator.

I see dreams as completely obtainable, so I am not the person to chat your wonders to if there is no action backing to it. To be frank, we are either planning to get to the dream or we need to be talking about something else. I am an introverted person with a mind that is very capable of creating. I am a master manifester. I get whatever I set my mind to because I clearly manifest it, I see the steps, and I take action. I feel into things, I move into them, I embody them. When someone presents an idea to me that is not logical, that they are not serious about, it often upsets me: *This cannot enter my mind.* What is thought, what is said, is what creates. If life is not a clear plan, you will continue to live in chaos. Growing is chaos, change is chaos, creating the plan is chaos. But stick to it and eventually it becomes clear and the golden path appears. Setting clear intentions and manifesting something into your reality is more than asking for an outcome; it is asking *how to get there* and paying attention to the action steps that are presented to you to act upon. Taking those steps is new ground and will be uncomfortable. Everything new is both uncomfortable and exciting, so *which* will you focus on?

People often ask me about my success story. I have many stories. My life has been very full because I pay attention to all the small things. The small things make up the big things. This chapter is my success story. Living fulfilled is about mindset; it is about creating, it is about your outlook on life. We need to feed into global energy, not individualism. We are all important, we are all unique, but we live off the same water and air. We are connected. Stop worrying about *yourself* and get to work on *all*. Everything that is systematic within society and business, within your industry, can be learned; as I said, it is systematic, after all. Focus on how you can give more, and just do more of that!

If you desire to have something, to have power in this society, to have peace in your reality, to feel fulfilled with a purpose in your soul, here is what I recommend:

- Work on self-confidence. Study self-confidence vs self-esteem.
- Start to laugh at yourself. You do not have to be perfect. You are unique, so there is no comparison. Perfection is a hard one; I am a perfectionist, but I do jump into things in a very messy way. I think that with perfectionism, we like to "fix." Focus on the fix, focus on the bettering; we come back to the word "growth," and once again the solution to the agony of perfectionism can be found in enjoying the journey and taking pressure off yourself. Remember, you are unique and no one else does it the way you do. All the reward is in taking action, in giving energy.
- Imagine your life within a world of peace versus a world of chaos. Don't you want good for all? Wouldn't that benefit you more than only focusing on your own needs?

- Identify the "dream" job. What could you spend all your days doing? It may not equate to something that pays financially, but how can you weave it into your career? You do this by setting it as a core value.
- Identify what you don't like doing, and create a plan for how you can stop doing it. Wasting time is wasting your life-force energy. People say, "I am killing myself doing this" in regard to things they don't like, are not meant for, or are not good at. They don't know how right they are . . .
- Start adding value to five people a day: pay them a compliment, share a joke, lend a helping hand, ask a question, support their business, and provide value and knowledge when they may need it or ask for it.
- Find mentors. While you are growing, you are still going to need approval, direction, and support. As much as we are found on our journey, we are just as lost; it is a continuous practice of seeking and finding. The goal is not to arrive but rather to experience and expand. Only focus on the guidance of the people who are where you want to be. We also can't do everything ourselves, so refer up to the "stop doing what you don't like" tip. We need mentors and support people throughout our entire journey so we can be the best we can be. We all have our own zone of genius.
- Read more books, ask more questions, attend more conferences. Learn more about sociology and global issues, and try to understand other people — I know it is hard! But we are all connected, we are much the same, so understanding others is the path to understanding more about yourself.
- Spend your money, and earn your money, better. Money is a tangible form of energy. When you support good companies and products, your energy is raised. When you work for or create good ethical business, your energy shoots to a very high frequency! When we support greed-centred companies, or act in a selfish or fake way, our energy / money goes into a bank to be confined, to be stored away from us, with restrictions on how, or if ever, we can use it. It does not come back out to the global energy grid. Greed-centred people and companies take cheap solutions, they rob energy, they keep people at a low frequency. They leech. When we support the wrong companies, act in a selfish manner, or have low frequency people around us, we are actually taking away from our self and the people we love — which affects everyone.
- If you do good business and provide needed products and services, you deserve to be paid. You deserve energy so you can keep doing more good things. If you aren't receiving enough, you likely aren't giving properly, you aren't showing up and being the energy the Universe is requiring you to be. It is give and take. Do not feel bad about receiving tangible energy for the work you do, and do not be scarce about letting it go. Do not let people take your energy for granted, and do not let them steal it or hold it. Do not let people be leeches and don't be a leech yourself.

By doing all of the above, you have taken major action. You have created momentum! You are changing the course of your timeline. By approaching your life from this energetic level, you are able to seek out what you truly need and will be ready to take the action required of you.

It's time to do ALL the things!

It is time to do all the things that you desire. Take the time you need to get to a good energetic state. Heal yourself so you can be a vessel for others. If you feel you have a good sense of self-esteem, if you are past expectations and are beginning to simply BE, you will realize you have the time to live out many stories at once. We were born to grow, and it is time we take responsibility for our life, our world, our society. We are all meant to play a bigger role. If we don't grow, if we do not share knowledge, if we don't gain what we are meant to from this experience here on earth, it is believed that we loop. We don't move on to the next dimension (fourth or fifth) or to the heavens, or to wherever it is you are going next. We *are* here for a reason. We are here to learn, to experience, to give, to become better, to survive, to be worthy and ready of moving into a higher level of consciousness.

~ I would like to acknowledge all the people in the world who are suffering at the hand of someone else. The rest of the world feels you, and we are going to do something about it. I want to acknowledge the power within each and every one of us reading this book, and to use this space to encourage you to be strong for others. If every person takes care of one other person, we will all be taken care of. Let's write a new world, together.

Timeless Practice:

◇— It's Time To Write A Piece Of Your Story —◇

To explore a writing program based on the teachings of this book, please join me at www.gbrsociety.com.

Contribution and being part of a community is how every successful and influential person lives. It's the way of true wealth.

Begin by realizing your unique and individual worth, discover your words and wisdom in this chapter, take a photo, and share it with us. See the power of it all. Hashtag #deartime and tag @gbrpublishing. We've got you! Welcome!

_____

_____

_____

_____

_____

_____

Timeless Practice:

Timeless Practice:

GOLDEN BRICK ROAD
PUBLISHING HOUSE

Locking arms and helping each other down their Golden Brick Road

At Golden Brick Road Publishing House, we lock arms with ambitious people and create success through a collaborative, supportive, and accountable environment. We are a boutique shop that caters to all stages of business around a book. We encourage women empowerment, and gender and cultural equality by publishing single author works from around the world, and creating in-house collaborative author projects for emerging and seasoned authors to join.

Our authors have a safe space to grow and diversify themselves within the genres of poetry, health, sociology, women's studies, business, and personal development. We help those who are natural born leaders, step out and shine! Even if they do not yet fully see it for themselves. We believe in empowering each individual who will then go and inspire an entire community. Our Director, Ky-Lee Hanson, calls this: The Inspiration Trickle Effect.

If you want to be a public figure that is focused on helping people and providing value, but you do not want to embark on the journey alone, then we are the community for you.

To inquire about our collaborative writing opportunities or to bring your own idea into fruition, reach out to us at:

www.goldenbrickroad.pub

Connect with our authors and readers at GBRSociety.com